Discovering Leviticus, Numbers & Deuteronomy

THE GUIDEPOSTS HOME BIBLE STUDY PROGRAM

Floyd W. Thatcher   *General Editor*
Robin White Goode   *Associate Editor*
Bob E. Patterson   *Technical Consultant*

Leviticus, Numbers & Deuteronomy

Discovering Leviticus, Numbers & Deuteronomy   Gary Demarest
What This Scripture Means to Me   Leslie Williams
Cover Artist   Ben Wohlberg
Map   Janice Gibson

DISCOVERING LEVITICUS, NUMBERS & DEUTERONOMY

The Guideposts Home Bible Study Program

GUIDEPOSTS®

Carmel   New York   10512

The photographs on the pages below were reproduced with the permission of the following photographers:

Bruce Cresson: 30, 31, 53, 77, 78, 94, 106 (*top and bottom*), 116, 117, 127, 198 (*bottom*).
William La Sor: 120, 144, 155, 165, 195, 198 (*top*).

The Guideposts Home Bible Study Program
Leviticus, Numbers & Deuteronomy
1. Discovering Leviticus, Numbers & Deuteronomy
2. My Working Bible
3. Knowing More About Leviticus, Numbers & Deuteronomy

Contents

Publisher's Introduction

In our studies now we will gain an overview of three little-known-and-studied books of our Bible. Yet, an understanding of what is being said and what is happening in these books will enrich our spiritual lives and make the Scripture as a whole come alive in a new way. All three of these books are widely quoted in the New Testament.

Leviticus is a book of worship. Its key word is "holiness"—its importance is stressed by the fact that it appears over eighty times in the book! With careful attention to detail God spells out through Moses instructions for worship and for behavior as people of God.

It is true, of course, that many of the rituals and symbols will seem strange to us. Yet as we come to understand them even a little bit, we can then better convert their deepest meaning to our own Christian pilgrimage. In many ways, the key to a better understanding of our New Testament Book of Hebrews is found in gaining a better understanding of Leviticus.

There are many lessons here for us as twentieth-century Christians, but chief among them is the importance of our worship. It was vital to the people of

Israel in the Sinai wilderness and in their ultimate occupation of Canaan. We come to a better understanding here of the importance of worship in the "wilderness" of our daily lives.

As we shall see, the Book of Numbers is far more interesting and exciting than its title would indicate. Actually, what we have here is almost forty years of very important history. But even more important is the ongoing drama of God's care and direction of His people. The Book of Numbers begins at the foot of Mount Sinai and ends at Mount Nebo and the invasion point east of the Jordan River across from the Canaanite city of Jericho.

Traveling with the people of Israel throughout all of those years gives us much more than historical and cultural insights. There are, instead, powerful spiritual lessons to be learned that have direct application to our Christian walk. The Apostle Paul emphasized this truth to the new Christians in Corinth when he referred to the wilderness travels of the Hebrews. After reminding his readers of the wilderness events of the people of Israel, Paul wrote, "Now all these things happened unto them for examples: and they are written for our admonition" (1 Cor. 10:11).

Like those first-century Christians in Corinth, we, too, will learn from the story of our spiritual ancestors and how God led them and cared for them over three thousand years ago.

The third book overviewed in these lessons is the one with a strange name—Deuteronomy. The meaning of the title is "second law" or "repetition of the law." The reason for this title is that we find in Chapters 12 through 26 a digest of much of the Law that was previously given in Exodus, Leviticus, and Numbers.

The ancient Hebrews, camped as they were with the Promised Land in sight, needed to be reminded by Moses of God's rules for worship and life.

For the most part the Book of Deuteronomy is made up of three major addresses given by Moses. These are masterpieces of thought and oratory. In them we catch a vision of the drama of God at work among His people. His redemptive patience with the people of Israel and His meticulous guidance of them are constantly reassuring to us.

As we read the words of the Lord through Moses, we get a new sense of the greatness of the man described by the Deuteronomy writer in these words, "And there arose not a prophet since in Israel like unto Moses, whom the Lord knew face to face" (34:10).

In Moses, the central human character in all eight lessons of our study, we have a model for our life and worship. His beginnings give us the clue to his long and useful life. The writer of the Book of Hebrews simply says, "By faith Moses, when he was come to years, refused to be called the son of Pharaoh's daughter; Choosing rather to suffer affliction with the people of God, than to enjoy the pleasures of sin for a season" (11:24–25).

Preface

I wish I could fully communicate the joy I've experienced in researching and writing these studies in Leviticus, Numbers, and Deuteronomy. To borrow a phrase coined by C. S. Lewis, I have been "surprised by joy."

And why has this been a surprise? Partly because I've never studied these writings with the depth and intensity I brought to this project. Looking back almost forty years to my seminary training, the Old Testament and I got off to a bad start. For a long time I blamed my professors, but I have since come to accept my own responsibility for what, all too long, was a serious deficiency in my understanding of the Old Testament.

Once I realized the crucial importance of overcoming that deficiency, I began to take my study of the Old Testament as seriously as I always had the New Testament. And I can tell you that the Bible came alive to me as never before!

I recall a shop-worn cliché that expresses an important truth, "The New Testament is in the Old *concealed,* the Old is in the New *revealed."* While the history of Old Testament interpretation abounds in fanciful "discoveries" of hidden truths couched in allegories or typology, today's student has the challenge and joy of sorting out previous interpretations in the light of our rapidly expanding understanding of ancient cultures and customs in the world of Israel's history from roughly 2,000 B.C. to 150 B.C. Archaeological, linguistic, cultural, and historical research are continually enriching our ability to expand our understanding of the life and times of ancient Israel, and thus of the Old Testament.

It is increasingly clear to me that there are two fundamental errors to be avoided by the layperson who wishes to benefit from the Old Testament without becoming involved in the demanding rigors of the several disciplines related to Old Testament scholarship.

The first is what I call the "historical" error: reading the Old Testament primarily as ancient history. I have a hunch that many folks give the Old Testament a wide berth because they really aren't all that enthusiastic about ancient Middle East history. But even those who read the Old Testament from that standpoint will be disappointed, for the purpose of the Old Testament writers was not to record history for future generations. Their purpose was to record the mighty acts of God in their lives.

The clear witness of the writers of the Old Testament was to their passionate conviction that God was very much present and active in the affairs and destinies of peoples and nations. We may not always understand their perceptions of some of the specific ways in which they understood God to be at work, but we will always be aware of their unswerving faith in God's presence and faithful love.

And isn't this a message much needed by us today? For us who are so conditioned to a rationalism grounded in mechanical views of causes and effects, we do well to keep a central place in our thinking for the God of creation and history who is present and active, always working in love and justice.

The Old Testament writings, especially these books that we are studying, ring with the passion of people who are aware that God has spoken to them and that He is present and active in their midst. We need to share that belief and passion in our day as well. At times when I wonder where God is and what He is doing, I do well to review the stubborn faith of the writers of the Old Testament throughout their long and troubled history.

The second error to avoid is what I call the "spiritual": reading the Old Testament as a source of direct messages from God quite apart from its history and setting. An example of this is found in the prevailing interpretations of the Book of Leviticus in the eighteenth and nineteenth centuries. All of the sacrifices and forms of worship were read as "types" of Christ, with little attention to the meaning that the worship had for the people in their time. It was fashionable to see who could come up with the greatest number of typologies.

Allegorical treatments also abound in this way of reading the Old Testament. Most everything becomes a symbol of something in our lives and times. While the lessons gained may be interesting and helpful, the danger is that in not taking the history seriously enough, we miss the deeper understanding and meaning of God's continuing self-disclosure to the people of the Covenant.

God was dealing with real people in real times and places. Only when we have tried to live in their history, their struggles, their joys, their sorrows, can we hope to experience God as they did. That Christ will come, and fulfill all of the promises, dreams, and hopes given to them by God, we well know. But to move to the end of the story too quickly deprives us of the ultimate appreciation of the meaning of Jesus.

For more than twenty-five years, I've been teaching my "Pastor's Bible Class" on Tuesday and Wednesday mornings. I would continue these classes if there were only two of us in a phone booth, because I have learned more in the teaching than anyone could have in the listening and discussions. I regard the consistent discipline of preparing in order to lead others into a deeper understanding of a biblical passage to be one of life's most joyous adventures.

The joy that I have experienced in preparing these lessons is great. I urge you to find some friends whom you might be able to lead to a deeper understanding of these books of the Bible with the help of this guide. And even if you use this guide only personally, study *as though* you were preparing to teach someone else. You'll find such study richly rewarding!

I pray that these three ancient books of the Bible will bring you the joy, meaning, and challenge that they have brought to me.

LESSON 1
Leviticus 1–16

How Should We Worship?

Dear Lord, Grant me wisdom, insight, and understanding as I grow in Your love. AMEN.

Leviticus has had a most unusual and unfortunate history. At one time, it was the first book studied by Jewish children in the synagogue. But among contemporary Christians, it may be the least read and known book of the Bible. And it's not too difficult to understand why this is so.

You have every right to raise questions as to why you should study Leviticus. What do the rituals for the animal and grain sacrifices of ancient Israel have to do with my worship of God? What do detailed regulations about ritual cleanness and uncleanness have to do with my walk with God? What kind of God required such severe penalties for what might seem to us to be honest errors in the conduct of worship?

Is Leviticus just to be seen as ancient history, little more than a record of a part of Israel's religious development? Or should we just read it to see what stories might have possible application in today's world? Or does this part of Scripture, like the rest of the Bible, have permanent and timely meaning and value for us today?

It is my deep conviction and personal experience that Leviticus has dynamic and profound meaning as the Word of God as much for us today as it did for those folks long ago for whom it was first written.

Let's start where it starts. "And the Lord called unto Moses, and spake unto him out of the tabernacle of the congregation, saying . . ." (1:1). This phrase occurs in almost the same form fifty-six times in the twenty-seven chapters of Leviticus. Whatever else we are aware of when we read Leviticus, let us be conscious that we are listening in on what God was saying to the people through Moses. Other than the narrative material in Chapters 8–10 and one short story (24:10–23), everything in Leviticus is recorded as God's direct word to Moses.

You will remember that after the Law was given on Mount Sinai (Exod. 20), Moses was given detailed instructions by God for the building of the Tabernacle, the clothing and ordination of Aaron and his sons as priests, and the basic form that their worship was to take. You might find it helpful to stop a few minutes and read the instructions given in Exodus 25–31 and 36–40 because Leviticus is a continuation of the story begun in Exodus in which God is speaking to Moses.

There's little point in speculating as to how God spoke to Moses. We need not necessarily think that Moses heard an audible voice, nor that he was some kind of recording device receiving Divine dictation. What makes Leviticus wondrous and awesome is that we have messages from God communicated directly through Moses.

In our two lessons on Leviticus, we will learn about worship and about life. In Chapters 1–16, the central theme is the worship of God. Chapters 17–26 deal primarily with the quality of life that is to flow out of the worship of God.

In Leviticus we find no separation between worship and life. The formal worship of God is always seen as essential to life that is truly human. Such worship shapes the style and quality of the lives of the worshipers. And an authentic human life must be grounded in worship.

In a period of our church life when participation in worship is regarded by many believers merely as an option, the central message of the Book of Leviticus needs to be heard and acted upon. And to those who plan and lead worship either routinely or carelessly, its message comes as a stern rebuke.

Worship: Optional or Imperative? (Chapters 1–7)

As we learn in our reading and study in the Book of Exodus, the center for Israel's worship for many years was the Tabernacle. By our standards, the building was quite rustic, and because of the semi-nomadic style of life that was to be Israel's for many years, it was portable in design. It could be moved readily when the children of Israel under God's guidance broke camp for a new location. Their place of worship was always with them and located in the very center of the camp.

The Place of Worship: The Tabernacle

Let's take a moment to refresh our memories and review the structure and setting of the Tabernacle (Exod. 25–28; 35–40). Inside the east gate, the only entrance to the Court, stood the Brazen Altar on which the priests offered sacrifices morning and evening. Between the Brazen Altar and the Tabernacle structure itself was the Brass Laver in which the priests washed their hands and feet before performing further acts of worship.

The Tabernacle itself dominated the Court. The skeletal structure of the Tabernacle consisted of a rectangle framework of interlocking, trellislike boards made of acacia wood. It measured approximately forty-five feet long, fifteen feet wide, and fifteen feet high. The covering was made up of ten curtains of finely woven material—blue, purple, and scarlet with embroidered cherubim. Over this was a protective covering made of ram and goat skins.

The Tabernacle was divided into two rooms. The first was the Holy Place in which were positioned the Golden Candlestick, the Table of Shewbread, and the Altar of Incense. Immediately behind the Holy Place was a smaller room called the Holy of Holies,

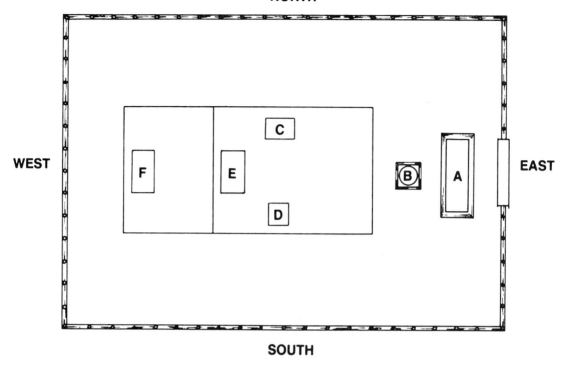

NORTH

WEST

EAST

SOUTH

An artist's impression of the layout of the Tabernacle and court. The door to the Tabernacle complex always faced east. Inside the gate was the Brazen Altar (A). Between the Brazen Altar and the Holy Place was the Laver (B). The first room in the Tabernacle was the Holy Place; its furnishings were the Table of Shewbread (C) on the north wall; the Golden Lampstand (D) on the south wall; and the Golden Altar of Incense (E) which stood next to the curtain that separated the Holy Place from the Holy of Holies. The inner room was the Holy of Holies, and its only item of furniture was the Ark of the Covenant (F).

which contained just one item of furniture: the Ark of the Covenant. Only the High Priest entered the Holy of Holies, and then just once each year on the Day of Atonement (Lev. 16).

The Offerings

In Chapters 1 through 7 of our Scripture for this lesson, we find instructions on the types of sacrifices to be offered. Five kinds of offerings are mentioned—

each with a different purpose. But central to all of these is the acceptance of the reality and seriousness of sin as causing separation from God. The five offerings described are the burnt offering, the meal or grain offering ("meat" in KJV), the peace offering, the sin offering, and the trespass offering. All of the offerings, with the exception of the meal, required the killing (sacrifice) of a live animal—a bull or sheep or goat or even doves and pigeons.

The animals to be sacrificed were to be the personal property of the worshiper. They were to be unblemished—perfect in every way. Nothing but the finest could be used in the sacrificial worship of God. We also learn in our Scripture lesson that not only were careful instructions given to the worshiper for each of the offerings (1:1–6:7), but detailed instructions were also spelled out for the officiating priests (6:8–7:38). In other words, the procedure and order for worship, even in the rugged desert wilderness, was of primary importance. Worship then and worship now are never to be casual or haphazard!

The Burnt Offering

The instructions for the worshiper bringing a burnt offering are found in Chapter 1:1–17, and the instructions for the priests are found in Chapter 6:8–13.

This was the basic and most familiar of the offerings. In the instructions to the priests we read, "The fire shall ever be burning upon the altar; it shall never go out" (6:13). While we're not given the reason for this continual fire, some believe that it was to be kept burning because the first burnt offerings were lit by a fire that came "from before the Lord" (9:24).

Most certainly, the perpetual flames of the burnt offerings were a constant reminder to the people that their consecration must be renewed daily, for this offering was essentially an expression of commitment and dedication to God. It is significant, I believe, that this was the only offering that was consumed completely by the fire. With the others, as we shall see, part of the offering was burned and part was eaten by either priests or the worshiper.

If you haven't already done so, I suggest that you

stop for a few moments and read the Scriptures describing this offering. As we reflect on this ancient act of worship, we are reminded of our own need to continually renew our commitment to God. It is true, of course, that our renewal doesn't require animal sacrifice, simply because Christ on the cross "offered one sacrifice for sins for ever. . . . For by one offering he hath perfected for ever them that are sanctified" (Heb. 10:12, 14). Yet, we today have the same need to keep the fires of our devotion burning as we offer our daily sacrifice of time, energy, and money.

The Leviticus writer makes a point of telling us that when the Hebrews took an animal to the priests for sacrifice, it was done voluntarily and the worshiper was personally identified with the offering: "he shall offer it of his own *voluntary will*. . . . And he shall put his hand upon the head of the burnt offering [on the head of the animal]; and it shall be accepted for him" (1:3–4, italics mine).

These two principles are very important. Our offerings to God—time, money, talents—are to be given voluntarily and gladly. Our service, whatever form it takes, is to be given with enthusiasm. When Paul wrote to his friends in Corinth about the importance of giving for the Lord's work, he worded it this way, "Every man according as he purposeth in his heart, so let him give; not grudgingly, or of necessity: for God loveth a cheerful giver" (2 Cor. 9:7).

Then, there is the importance of our being personally identified with our offerings and gifts to God. The ancient Hebrew worshiper did this by placing his hands on the head of the animal to be sacrificed. In contrast, our identification with our offerings to God becomes real as we give of our very selves to Him.

Paul must have had this burnt offering in mind when he wrote these words to his Christian friends in Rome, "I beseech you therefore, brethren, by the mercies of God, that ye present your bodies a living sacrifice, holy, acceptable unto God, which is your reasonable service" (Rom. 12:1). The Apostle used the same Greek word for "service" here that would have been used for the bringing of a burnt offering.

As the ancient Hebrews renewed their devotion and commitment to God through the burnt offering, so let us daily consecrate ourselves anew to Him by bringing our bodies—all that we are and have and hope to be—to God as a *living* sacrifice. In doing that we can be certain we are bringing pleasure to God even as the smoke from the burnt offerings arose and was "a sweet savour unto the Lord" (1:13).

The Grain Offering

The instructions for the worshiper with the grain or meal offering are found in Chapter 2:1–16, and the instructions for the priests are found in Chapter 6:14–23.

The name of this offering provides an interesting example of how the meaning of words can change over a period of time. When the King James Version of our Bible was published in the seventeenth century, the word "meat" was used generically for anything that was eaten. In contemporary usage, of course, meat refers to the flesh of living creatures—animals, fish, or fowl. It is more accurate to refer to this offering as a grain or meal or cereal offering.

Since the grain offering always followed the daily burnt offering (Num. 28:1–6), it is not surprising that it is listed here immediately after the burnt offering. Along with the burnt offering and the peace offering, the grain offering is one of the three sacrifices that produce "a sweet savour unto the Lord" (1:9; 2:2; 3:5).

Since many people, especially after the Israelites occupied Canaan, made their living agriculturally, the grain offering enabled them to bring an offering to God that was the fruit of their labor. Perhaps the farmer, more than others, is always reminded that everything we have is a gift from God. But this offering also required the labor of the farmer to grind it into fine flour, so that it represented both God's gift and human labor.

The actual Hebrew word used for this offering meant a present or a tribute or a memorial. It was given as a gift to God for no other reason than to bring Him a gift. In this sense, the grain offering has significance for us today. While we are no longer required to bring such offerings to our place of worship because of Christ's complete sacrifice on the Cross, we can still experience the same joy as the ancient worshiper in giving our gifts to God without thought of personal gain.

In bringing the grain offering as a gift to God, the Hebrews were also bringing gifts to the priests, for part of the offering was burned as "a sweet savour" to God, and the rest became the bread, the basic staple, for the priests (2:2, 3). What a delightful picture. Here was an offering—a gift—that brought both pleasure to God and sustenance to others!

Giving for the sheer joy of giving—to God and to others—has become a vanishing art in the late twentieth century. I recently attended a seminar in which there was somber discussion about the impact of possible changes in tax laws upon charitable giving. The consensus was that giving is frequently tied to "the cost of giving."

How sad! How different it was with a congregation of poor black Christians in Zimbabwe with whom I had worshiped and preached. After my sermon, the pastor spoke to the people in their language, and an offering was received. My interpreter whispered to me that the offering was to be given to me. My knee-jerk reaction was either to decline the offering or to direct it to some local need. My interpreter told me emphatically that I was to do neither. The reason soon became clear.

When the elders brought the offering to me, the pastor said, "My dear brother, in our culture we have a tradition in our homes to always have an extra chair and plate at our table so we will have the joy of providing a meal to any friend or stranger who might arrive at mealtime. Since you are one and we are many, you cannot come into all of our homes. But we want the joy of providing a meal for you. Please accept this offering as our gift to you."

The happy smiles on the faces of those dear brothers and sisters in giving something to me is indelibly etched into my memory. The offering was just enough to buy a cheeseburger and a milkshake at the

Harare Holiday Inn, but that meal will always rank as the most sumptuous I've ever eaten!

The Peace Offering

The instructions for the worshiper with the peace offering are found in Chapter 3:1–17, and the instructions for the priests are found in Chapter 7:11–38.

As we read about the peace offering in Chapters 3 and 7 of our Scripture lesson, we find an interesting difference between this one and the others. When the offering was made, part of it was consumed in flames for the Lord, part of it was eaten by the priests, and the main portion was returned to the worshiper to be enjoyed with his family and friends.

The peace offering was not presented daily but was made on special occasions when the worshiper wanted to offer special thanksgiving to God (7:12), make a special vow (7:16), or simply present a voluntary offering (7:16).

All three occasions called for a party, a time to celebrate with family and friends. Unfortunately, many people today have difficulty in linking worship with parties. Any thought of celebration, laughter, or sheer enjoyment is usually checked at the front door before entering the sanctuary for worship. To be sure, there are times for solemn confession, for quiet reflection, and for serious admonition. But the peace offering reminds us that there is a time for festive celebration and fellowship in the rhythms of worship.

In describing this offering, the Leviticus writer stresses repeatedly the prohibition against eating any of the fat or blood from this offering (3:17; 7:22–27). There is also a restriction against eating any of the flesh of the animal on or after the third day (7:17). These prohibitions deserve a closer look.

Both the blood and the fat were reserved for God. A well-known paragraph later in Leviticus expresses this idea, "For the life of the flesh is in the blood: and I have given it to you upon the altar to make an atonement for your souls: for it is the blood that maketh an atonement for the soul. Therefore I said unto the children of Israel, No soul of you shall eat blood, neither shall any stranger that sojourneth among you eat blood" (17:11–12). For the Hebrews, the blood was God's means for the removal or covering of sin. This simply meant then that the blood was set aside exclusively for God. And it was this principle that became the basis for the laws of *kosher* in the Hebrew community.

The restriction against eating fat wasn't because the ancient Hebrews were concerned about cholesterol or because they were worried about an excessive consumption of fatty foods. Quite the contrary! For them the fat was thought to be the most valuable part of the animal. In fact, they raised a special kind of sheep that grew an exceptionally fat tail which weighed in some instances as much as twenty-five pounds. This was considered a rare delicacy, much like our prime rib or filet mignon. The best was reserved for God.

The third restriction placed on the eating of the peace offering sacrifice was that it was to be consumed the same day preferably, but none was to be eaten on or after the third day. The reasoning behind this restriction was very practical. There was no refrigeration out there in the desert or in Canaan. Spoiled meat could wreak havoc on the camp. It was just good sense to destroy any of the meat from the peace offering after the second day.

The Sin Offering

The description of the sin offering is found in Chapters 4:1 to 5:13 and in 6:24–30. Like the burnt offering and the grain offering, the sin offering was made regularly though not as frequently, according to the provision outlined in Numbers 28 and 29. (You will notice that the King James Version uses the term "trespass offering" in Chapter 5:6, but it is the sin offering that is being discussed.) This sacrifice was considered the principle offering for atonement—the forgiveness of sin, the restoration of a right relationship between God and people. Sin separates; it is disruptive. For the ancient Hebrew, the sin offering provided forgiveness and through it they were made right with God.

Before going any further it is important to emphasize that the provisions of the sin offering covered only inadvertent sins—the unintentional infractions of the Law. In the Book of Leviticus a clear distinction is drawn between inadvertent sin and deliberate sin. In the regular sacrificial system there was no provision made for deliberate acts of sin. Expiation from acts of deliberate sin was available only on the annual Day of Atonement, which will be discussed toward the end of this lesson.

In contrast to this, the dramatic provision for the forgiveness and atonement of *all our sins* through the death of Jesus Christ on the cross exceeds all provisions made in ancient Israel. Imagine, if you can, the feeling of the Jewish reader in reading John's words, "My little children, these things write I unto you, that ye sin not. And if any man sin, we have an advocate with the Father, Jesus Christ the righteous: and he is the propitiation [the atoning sacrifice, the remedy] for our sins: and not for our sins only, but also for the sins of the whole world" (1 John 2:1–2).

It is with this in mind that the ancient sin offering described in our lesson is a model for us of the continuing need for confession. Whether in the liturgical prayer of confession in a service of Christian worship or in a personal prayer while kneeling beside one's bed at the end of the day, we need to confess our sins and receive God's forgiveness. And in doing so we have the promise, "If we confess our sins, he is faithful and just to forgive us our sins, and to cleanse us from all unrighteousness" (1 John 1:9).

The Trespass Offering

The description of the trespass offering is found in Chapters 5:14–6:7 and 7:1–10.

The trespass or guilt offering is closely related to the sin offering. The difference was that the trespass offering covered a particular kind of sin: (1) "sin through ignorance, in the holy things of the Lord" (5:15); (2) unknowingly doing "things which are forbidden to be done by the commandments of the Lord" (5:17); and (3) fraudulent actions against another person's property or falsely swearing under oath in such cases (6:1).

The first two of these sins were generally regarded as having to do with sacred property in the place of worship—eating the holy food or stealing from the tithes. The third type mentioned above has to do with the property rights of others and ranges from outright robbery to subtle chicanery, including such injustices as not paying a fair wage or taking advantage of another person.

The trespass offering called for restitution to be made. But then, after restitution had been made, there was an additional penalty of twenty percent assessed (6:5). The trespass offering was a reminder that sins against the rights and property of others was, and is, a sin against God.

But for the Christian, Christ is the perfect trespass offering. He not only covered our sins, but He redeemed us and restored us. He made complete reparation and amends for our sin. When we have sinned against another person, the lesson of the trespass offering is a reminder to confess that sin and make restitution; as we do, we will experience reconciliation both with God and the other person.

Perhaps one of the most beautiful examples in modern times of how openness and confession and restitution can give spiritual dynamism to the Christian church is in Uganda. Recently I joined with twenty thousand Ugandan Christians in the celebration of the fiftieth anniversary of the East Africa Revival. This great movement of the Holy Spirit began in Rwanda in 1935. For all these years its emphasis has been "Walking in the Light."

Every ten years since the outbreak of that great renewal movement there has been a celebration of the continuing work of the Holy Spirit. The Jubilee celebration I attended had been postponed from 1985 to 1986. People came on foot, riding bicycles, or in open trucks and buses. They camped and slept where they could and took their meals in local schools or the hospital.

That great mass of people joined in celebration of a unity in the Spirit. There was a grand spirit of reconciliation made possible through confession and restitution. There was no sign of bickering and in-fighting in this great outpouring of Christian love. This indeed was the message of the trespass offering for ancient Israel.

Welcome to the Priesthood (Chapters 8–10)

As we read these three chapters in this ancient book of worship, we might be tempted just to see ourselves as spectators at the first—and rather strange to us—ordination service of a long line of priests beginning with Aaron and his sons. We've already mentioned that these chapters are the only narrative section in the Book of Leviticus, other than the section in 24:10–23. These particular chapters should be read as an extension of Exodus 28–29.

From the outset, the priesthood was not a matter of human choice. Aaron, Moses' older brother, was appointed by God through Moses, and all of his sons and descendants were priests unless barred by legal disabilities (Lev. 21:16–23). A person did not choose to be a priest.

The Primary Duties of the Priests

The priests had three primary duties. The first was to minister in the worship center—offering the sacrifices in the Tabernacle, and eventually in the Temple. Second, the priests were also the teachers of the people. It was their responsibility to keep the Law of God before the people. Third, the priests were to discover the will of God for the people by using the Urim and Thummim which had been placed in the Breastplate that was worn by Aaron, the high priest.

While we can't be certain as to what the Urim and Thummim were, two theories have prevailed. The theory preferred by most scholars is that they were two stones that had been painted white on one side and black on the other. When a decision regarding God's will about a matter was needed, the stones were thrown down on the ground. If the white side of each stone was facing up, the decision was yes. However, if the black side of each stone was up, the answer was no. If the white side of one stone was up and the black side of the other stone was up, there was no decision.

A theory not so widely held by students of Scripture is that the Urim and Thummim were sealed within the Breastplate and rested close to the heart of the high priest. Then, when the high priest needed to make a decision, he was guided by the presence of the Urim and Thummim by receiving an inner sense of what God wanted.

The use of the Urim and Thummim was only for making decisions that affected the children of Israel as a nation.

Representatives of the People Before God

As the priesthood developed into an office of central importance in the life of Israel, the priest was seen as representing the people before God. The prophets, on the other hand, spoke to the people on behalf of God. And during those periods in Israel's history when the priesthood became corrupt and self-indulgent, it was often the prophets who confronted them and called them to account. At the time of Jesus, for example, the priesthood was in sad disarray. The high priests were no longer descendants of Aaron but were political appointees.

When you read Chapter 10 of our Scripture lesson, it may have seemed that the punishment of Aaron's two sons, Nadab and Abihu, was unusually severe. But it is apparent that their actions represented an abuse of their ordination or consecration in defiance of God's instructions for worship. While we don't know for sure, it is possible the incense they used had not been prepared properly or they had started their own fires instead of using the fire from the altar as God had directed. But whatever it was that they did when they went to conduct worship in the Holy Place, it is clear they deliberately disobeyed the Lord's instructions. It was their way of saying to God and to the people, "We'll do it *our* way."

The Priesthood and the Twentieth-Century Christian

At this point, we would do well to ask ourselves, "What does all of this material on the Levitical priesthood have to do with us in our attempt to be Christian? Is this study merely an exercise in reliving the distant past just for the sake of accumulating trivia?"

Decidedly not. What we learn here has definite

application to us simply because of the electrifying words from the writer of 1 Peter, "Ye are a chosen generation, *a royal priesthood,* an holy nation, a peculiar people [a people that belong to God]" (2:9, italics mine).

Based on Peter's good news that we are priests, we may find it interesting and informative to take another look at the consecration service found in Chapter 8 of our Scripture lesson. This will enable us to see the application between then and now.

We're told right at the beginning of the consecration ceremonies in Leviticus that Israel's priests were chosen by God. And the writer of 1 Peter stresses the fact that we—all Christians—are chosen by God. Then we read that the consecration ceremonies opened with the washing—the cleansing—of the priests (8:6). As Christians and members of the *royal priesthood,* we too are cleansed. The writer of 1 John makes this clear with these words, "If we confess our sins, he is faithful and just to forgive us our sins, *and to cleanse us* from all unrighteousness" (1:9, italics mine)—our baptism attests to that reality.

Next, we're told that in the consecration ceremony the priests were given special clothing to be worn in the performing of their service of worship (8:7–9). In a similar fashion, when a person becomes a Christian, the old ways—the old garments—are set aside and we put on the new garments of compassion, kindness, humility, gentleness, and patience (Col. 3:12). In writing to the Christians in Ephesus, Paul also lists the protective clothing the Christian is to wear in the battle against sin (Eph. 6:10–18).

We then read that in addition to being washed and clothed, the priests were anointed with oil (8:12)—a constant reminder that they belonged to God. And for the Christian, the anointing with oil is a symbol of the anointing and presence of the Holy Spirit—the very presence of God within us. It is through our cleansing, the putting on of a new self, and the anointing presence of the Holy Spirit that our worship and service has meaning and significance.

Finally, the various sacrifices were offered in the

ABOVE AND OPPOSITE. Two views of rugged Mount Sinai. Here we see a portion of the trail leading to the top. The picture opposite was taken near the top of Mount Sinai. It was in Sinai's peaks where the Lord met with Moses and gave him instructions for the Tabernacle and worship.

consecration ceremonies with Moses officiating. In the midst of that sacrificial ritual Moses did what seems to be a strange thing. He took some of the blood from the ram sacrifice "and put it upon the tip of Aaron's right ear, and upon the thumb of his right hand, and upon the great toe of his right foot." Then we read that this same procedure was followed with each of Aaron's sons (8:23–24). What a wonderfully dramatic way of saying that the priests were consecrated *to listen, to work,* and *to walk* with God!

Welcome to the priesthood of all believers!

Clean and Unclean (Chapters 11–15)

As we are beginning to see, I am sure, the Book of Leviticus is really a Worship Handbook or Guide, and the key word for the entire book is *holiness*. These

30

five chapters in our Scripture lesson open with what will be the central theme of the rest of the book: that you may "put difference between holy and unholy, and between unclean and clean" (10:10). Or, a more up-to-date way to put it is that we are to learn the difference between the sacred and the profane—between the pure and the impure.

As we attempt to read and understand these chapters in our Scripture lesson, it is like stepping into a strange and different world. Yet for those ancient people who first heard these instructions it all made a lot of sense, and as we shall see the symbolism is not only rich but immensely practical.

In Chapter 11 we find dietary and health laws that were vital to a people in a hot, desert climate who were several thousand years away from even the dream of refrigeration. Procedures for the purification from "uncleanness" after childbirth are spelled out in Chapter 12. Instructions are given in Chapters 13 and 14 for handling the "uncleanness" of skin diseases. And Chapter 15 spells out steps that are to be taken in the cleansing of "bodily issues"—discharges related to sexual functions and the genital area.

What Difference Do These Rules Make to Us?

Again, we ask ourselves, "What difference does this make to us?" I think it does make a difference, but to understand it even a little, we need to begin with the fundamental idea on which all of these instructions were based—the idea of *holiness.* God is holy! This means that He is "the wholly Other"—One who is different from all others and everything else; He is perfect in His wisdom, power, goodness, purity, justice, and truth.

The root idea of holiness is *separateness.* This means that human beings who are not holy are separated from God. And in the imagery of the Book of Leviticus, the unholy—the unclean—cannot touch anything that is clean, and that which is profane can in no way relate to the sacred.

Preparation for Worship

It is only as we grasp, however loosely, this understanding of the holiness of God that we can in any way comprehend the seriousness with which these ancient Hebrews regarded their worship over three thousand years ago. The Tabernacle was the place where God was present for them. It was God's Tent. And no one could approach God's Tent without being properly prepared. Every single detail—cleanliness, clothing, attitudes—had to be right. Approaching God was a serious and awesome matter in which nothing was treated lightly or left to chance.

I can identify in a rather distant and imperfect way with how the priests and the people must have felt when they approached the Tabernacle. When I was invited one time to participate in a special program at the White House in Washington, I gave a great deal of thought to my appearance. The shirt, tie, suit, and shoes that I wore were selected with care. Nothing was left to chance as I prepared for my visit to this very special place.

In reading about the care for detail that was so important to the worship of the children of Israel, and in reflecting on my reactions as I prepared to visit the White House, I have been reminded again of just how essential it is for us to be properly prepared for our worship of God, whether it be in a quiet time during the week in our homes or in the Lord's house on Sunday. Somehow I get the feeling that we are overly casual in our worship and approach to God. I believe there is a great need to regain a sense of the holiness of our Creator God who is also our heavenly Father.

To the people of ancient Israel, holiness was the supreme requirement that had to be met in order for them to worship God. The priests and the people had to be holy for their worship to have meaning. And the holiness referred to here was not unattainable, for the Leviticus writer gives us these words, "For I am the Lord your God: ye shall therefore sanctify [consecrate] yourselves, *and ye shall be holy;* for I am holy . . . ye shall therefore be holy, for I am holy" (11:44–45, italics mine).

For the people then and for us today, being holy does not mean that either they or we reach any stage of perfection. But it does mean that we are to be committed to always reach for that quality of holiness required of all who would enter into God's presence.

I believe that if we read this part of our Scripture lesson in light of all we've said so far, there will be no need to get bogged down with the details of the dietary and health laws that are listed here. These were just commonsense thinking for the Hebrews some three thousand years ago—but it is interesting that the principles behind certain of them have a very up-to-date sound.

Instead, we should reach out for the deeper meaning being conveyed. For me, there are two underlying principles woven into the fabric of this section of Scripture. The first involves the very close linkage between the spiritual and the physical. What we eat, how we take care of our bodies, personal cleanliness and sanitation—all are involved in our relationship with God and with other people.

There is a great deal of emphasis on health and fitness in our culture today in spite of the reports that our tendency toward fast food diets and our bad

Reach for the Deeper Meaning

eating habits are bad for us physically. Attention to diet and health for spiritual "fitness" was required of our Hebrew spiritual ancestors. In a similar fashion, if we are to be at our best for God, we need to be good stewards of our health.

The second principle that comes through here in our reading is that of "cleansing." You noticed, I am sure, that whenever a Hebrew man or woman was "unclean" and in isolation for whatever reason, God had made a provision for certain cleansing ceremonies. When these ceremonies had been observed, the person could come out of quarantine and was welcomed back into the social and worship life of the community.

I find both of these principles clearly emphasized in our New Testament Scriptures as well. To the Corinthian Christians who lived in a city widely known for its moral decadence, Paul wrote, "Know ye not that your body is the temple of the Holy Ghost which is in you, which ye have of God" (1 Cor. 6:19). There is no separation of body and spirit in the Christian life. There are indeed spiritual implications to the way in which we take care of our bodies. The writer of 1 John 1:9 also reminds us that God's grace in and through Jesus Christ provides complete cleansing and restoration.

The Day of Atonement (Chapter 16)

We come now to the central chapter of the Book of Leviticus which contains the detailed instructions for the ritual of sacrifices that were to be made once a year on the Day of Atonement. It was on this day that atonement was made for all the sins of individuals and of the nation that were not covered in the daily sacrificial system already described. On this day, with its special form of sacrifices and worship, forgiveness of sin became a reality for everyone and for the nation of Israel as a whole.

The Sacrifices and Cleansing

We won't note here every movement of the high priest on this special day—you will be aware of this in your reading. But you will note that the high priest's first act was to wash and cleanse himself and then to put on "holy garments" (16:4). Aaron then assembled a young bullock for the sin offering, a ram for the burnt offering, and two goats—one also for the sin offering and the other to "be presented alive before the Lord" (16:3–10).

On that day the high priest offered sacrifices for his sins and those of his family and for the sins of all the people. Provisions were made with each sacrificial offering for the high priest to enter the innermost sanctuary of the Tabernacle, the Holy of Holies. Other than on the Day of Atonement, once a year, no one entered this dwelling place of the Lord, and then only the high priest stepped within the veil.

With each sacrifice, we read that the high priest sprinkled some of the blood from the offering on the altar. Then, as a part of the sacrificial ritual, he also sprinkled blood in the Tabernacle itself and the Court of the Tabernacle as an act of cleansing. It would seem that even the sanctuary and Court of the Tabernacle needed cleansing because of their association with a sinful people.

The Scapegoat

Then came a most unique and colorful sacrifice. The Leviticus writer tells us that the goat which was "presented alive before the Lord" was brought out. As Aaron laid "both his hands upon the head of the live goat," he confessed "over him all the iniquities of the children of Israel, and all their transgressions in all their sins, putting them upon the head of the goat." When this was done, the goat was driven out into the wilderness, never to be seen again. In this highly symbolic act, we have a vivid and colorful picture of sin being not only covered but removed from the presence of the people forever (16:21–22). This scapegoat scene reminds us of Isaiah's prophetic words, "Surely he hath borne our griefs, and carried our sorrows. . . . All we like sheep have gone astray; we have turned every one to his own way; *and the Lord hath laid on him the iniquity of us all*" (Isa. 53:4, 6, italics mine).

The final ceremony on the Day of Atonement was enacted with Aaron once again dressed in his priestly robes, offering the burnt offering sacrifice as an "atonement for himself, and for all the people," and the remains from the sacrifice were taken outside the camp and burned (16:23–28).

A Statute Forever

So important was this day in the religious life of the Hebrews that God established it as a permanent institution. Quoting the Lord, the Leviticus author writes, "And this shall be a statute for ever unto you: that in the seventh month, on the tenth day of the month, ye shall afflict your souls [mortify, deny, humble], and do no work at all, whether it be one of your own country, or a stranger that sojourneth among you [a native Israelite or a foreigner]. For on that day shall the priest make an atonement for you, to cleanse you, that ye may be clean from all your sins before the Lord. It shall be a sabbath of rest unto you, and ye shall afflict your souls, *by a statute for ever*" (16:29–31, italics mine). And to make sure that the people understand, in the closing words of the chapter the Lord repeats Himself: *"And this shall be an everlasting statute* unto you, to make an atonement for the children of Israel for all their sins once a year" (16:34, italics mine).

To this day Jews have remembered those instructions. On Yom Kippur, the Day of Atonement, faithful Jews are in the synagogue asking God for forgiveness. It is the holiest day of the Jewish year. It is a time of repentance.

Good News for the Christian

For the Christian, the rich symbolism of the Day of Atonement takes form as we trace the words of the writer of the Book of Hebrews, Chapters 9 and 10. Here we have a commentary on the meaning of Christ's death as seen through the long history of the sacrificial system described in the Book of Leviticus. I urge you to read it again.

For the first-century Jewish Christian and for Christians of all time, the writer of the Book of Hebrews declares emphatically the good news: "But Christ being come an high priest of good things to come, by a greater and more perfect tabernacle, not made with hands, that is to say, not of this building; Neither by the blood of goats and calves, but by his own blood he entered in once into the holy place, having obtained eternal redemption for us. For if the blood of bulls and of goats, and the ashes of an heifer sprinkling the unclean, sanctifieth to the purifying of the flesh: How much more shall the blood of Christ, who through the eternal Spirit offered himself without spot to God, purge your conscience from dead works to serve the living God?" (Heb. 9:11–14).

For the ancient Hebrews, sacrifice for sin had to be repeated endlessly, and even the Day of Atonement was needed annually. But thanks be to God, "Christ was *once* offered to bear the sins of many" (Heb. 9:28, italics mine). In Christ, sin has been put away (Heb. 9:26).

Father God, What the blood of goats and bulls could never do, You did through the shed blood of the Lord Jesus: You have freed me from the power of sin, and allowed me to fellowship with You. Amen.

WHAT THIS SCRIPTURE MEANS TO ME
Leviticus 1—16

When I was ten, I went over to a friend's house to play. We were left with a sitter, and we played more rambunctiously than usual. We horsed around in their elegant living room, pushing and shouting in excited child's play.

Suddenly, before I could stop it, my hand brushed against an expensive crystal ashtray and it shattered on the floor. I looked at it in horror.

After I picked up the pieces, I sat down on the couch. I wasn't interested in playing any more. My insides felt like lead.

Finally, when the grownups came home, I rushed up to my friend's father and confessed my sin. "I'll buy you a new ashtray," I said through my tears, although I knew it would take years to pay for it.

Graciously he forgave me and told me he would replace the ashtray himself. On the way home, I felt lighthearted again.

As an adult, I have often felt the burden of sin. When I get angry, or when I envy a friend, or say something unkind, I often feel as if I have stones in my stomach until I confess it and try to make things right.

In this lesson, we see how God provided a way for the Israelites to become unburdened from their sins. Though the time had not yet come for Jesus to make His once-and-for-all sacrifice on the cross, God did not leave His people to suffer in the meantime. He provided the rituals of animal sacrifices so they wouldn't be separated from Him by their sin. God wanted them to grow in an understanding of Him, to become His children who one day would accept the promised Messiah.

As I reflect on the elaborate system of sacrifices described in our lesson, I am haunted by the question, "How can I be the kind of living sacrifice God wants and can use?" When I'm honest, I admit that any sacrifices I've made in my Christian pilgrimage have been insignificant. They shrink even more when compared to the sacrifice of an orphan boy in Vietnam, whose story I heard about recently.

He was six years old and had developed a blood disease. He needed a transfusion or he would die.

When the orphanage director heard the news, he gathered all the orphans together. "Our friend is very sick," he said, "and he will die unless somebody volunteers to give him blood." He looked around the room.

The sick boy wasn't popular. He had bullied the smaller children and teased the older ones. The children looked down at the floor.

The director repeated his plea. Finally one little boy reluctantly raised his hand.

At the hospital, the doctor stretched the young volunteer on a cot. When the nurse stuck his vein with a needle, he began to whimper.

"There, there," said the doctor. "It will soon be over."

As the nurse filled up tube after tube with his blood, the boy whimpered more loudly. When she finally took the needle out of his arm, he lay motionless on the cot, still whimpering.

The doctor knelt beside him and said gently, "What's the matter?"

Crying softly, the boy looked at him. "How long will it take me to die?" He didn't understand about blood transfusions.

Like Jesus on the cross, and like the sacrificial goats we read about in our lesson, the boy had offered his life for another.

This lesson tells us that God loves us and forgives our sins. He called the Israelites—and He calls us—into a relationship with Him. We can become living sacrifices for God by giving up our own desires, plans, and even our lives for His purpose.

LESSON 2
Leviticus 17–27

How Should We Live?

Father, Help me to walk in humble obedience to Your will, to demonstrate the holiness that allows me to be who I really am. AMEN.

As we move now into the last part of our study of the Book of Leviticus, we come to what is generally referred to as "The Holiness Code" (Chapters 17–27). In our last lesson we took a close look at the priesthood and the sacrificial system God had designed for the Hebrew people. Then we came to the grand climax in the Day of Atonement, the annual day of celebration and cleansing.

In all of these studies we have come to see that this rather obscure and little-known Old Testament book is crucial to our understanding of the full meaning of Christ's atoning death on the Cross. Because of this I think we can say with certainty that the Book of Leviticus gives us the basics for a better understanding of God and our relationship with Him as we discover it in the Bible.

In Leviticus we get an early picture of God as the God of grace and redemption. Here we see a God who meets the sincere worshiper with forgiveness. In addition we get a picture of what it means to be a whole person in relationship to the community of God's people—a needed antidote to the excessive individualism so prevalent in the twentieth-century western Christian community.

As we've seen, the central theme of the Book of Leviticus is holiness in worship and in life. It stresses that as people of God we are to walk humbly with Him in obedience to His will. Some interpreters have suggested that Chapters 1 through 16 are really a summary of the first part of the Golden Rule, "Thou shalt love the Lord thy God . . ." And the remaining chapters that we are coming to in this lesson apply the meaning of "and thou shalt love thy neighbor as thyself."

As we move now into our brief study of the Holiness Code, it will help to review just what is meant by "holiness." In speaking of the holiness of God we mean essentially that God is "wholly other." He is infinite in His love, goodness, justice, mercy, and power, and He instructs His people to be holy "for I am holy."

To the ancient Hebrew, holiness wasn't thought of as an impossible ideal, but as an immediate reality made possible by obedience to God in the power of His Spirit. The quest for holiness wasn't regarded as an effort to become something they were not, but rather to become who they really were. For them, obedience to God in worship and in life was not an effort to "achieve" God's grace and acceptance. Rather, it was an effort to live out in gratitude what God "had given them." So, the Holiness Code for the Hebrew was not observed in order to *become* holy, but in order to *demonstrate* the holiness that God had already placed within them.

Such being the case, we have to ask, "What about us today? Are we to keep each of these laws? Were they given for all times and places?" In response to these questions I have to say first of all that as we read Leviticus, it is absolutely clear that the laws described here were given by God to His people. Then as we read on, we're unable to locate anything that tells us these laws became inoperative.

But the plain fact of the matter is that neither Jews nor Christians today follow these rules as they are given in our Leviticus lessons. How do we account for that?

I think we find a clue to the answer in Jesus' Sermon on the Mount. It is true that He affirms the laws of the Hebrew Scriptures, but He also clearly calls for a change. At no point do we get the idea from Jesus' words in this sermon that He minimized in any way the demands of the Law for His listeners. Instead, it seems clear that Jesus is calling for His followers to move beyond the letter of the law to a greater responsibility. And while we aren't bound to observe certain of the specifics laid down by God for His people some three thousand years ago as they moved around the Sinai desert and then occupied the Land of Promise, the overriding principles that governed the giving of those laws—the holiness of God and His people—remain very much a part of our Christian tradition and our pilgrimage of faith in the high-tech world of the late twentieth century.

Holiness in Eating
(Chapter 17)

At first glance it might seem that the regulations in this part of our lesson are a continuation of the ceremonial rules related to clean and unclean food that we found in our last lesson (Chapter 11). But a closer look tells us that the emphasis here is primarily on holiness and not health. The particular regulations given here had a specific purpose—to make the Hebrews different in their way of life from the pagan people they would be in contact with on the Sinai Peninsula and in Canaan when they got there.

As we have already seen, the Hebrews' worship of God was an intimate part of their daily life-style. They were not guilty of separating the sacred from the secular the way we do. For them, everything was sacred, and every part of their life, including the preparation and eating of their food, was related to their daily worship. It is in this context that the Leviticus writer gives two important and timeless principles concerning the preparation and the consumption of meat.

Whenever an unblemished animal—ox, lamb, goat—was to be killed for food, it was first to be taken "to the door of the tabernacle of the congregation" where the priest accepted it as a peace offering to the Lord. The animal was killed and its blood was collected by the priest in a bowl. The blood was either sprinkled on the ground or on the sides of the Altar of Burnt Offering. The priest would burn the fat according to the instructions for the peace offering, and then take his allotted portion of the meat. The rest of the animal was returned to its owner who took it home as food for the family.

In other words, the killing of animals for food constituted a ritual of worship, symbolizing that all they had came from God. Apparently, though, some of the Hebrews were not following the prescribed pattern and were killing their animals outside of the camp and not at the Tabernacle as instructed.

We might wonder just why it was so important to go through this religious ritual every time they killed their livestock. Why were those who didn't follow the rules for the peace offering accused of offering "their sacrifices unto devils, after whom they have gone a whoring" (17:7)?

The answer to those questions begins to be clear when we understand that the pagan people in the Sinai Peninsula and in Canaan connected the killing of their livestock with degrading immoral acts of worship of their gods. The Hebrews were to be different from their neighbors. They were to look and act different. All of their life, including the killing of their livestock, was to center on their place of worship, the place where God was in their midst, and not outside the camp somewhere.

This Tabernacle-centered life-style of the Hebrews is a model for us. There are those who try to sell the idea that they can worship God on the golf course or while "communing with nature" just as well as they can in church; but I can't buy that. There are those, too, whose worship center is really "outside the camp" of their daily experiences instead of

Offered First at the Tabernacle

at the center. It is to such thinking, I believe, that this part of our lesson speaks. Everything in life is sacred. God and our worship of Him is to be central.

Our protection against slipping away, even ever so slowly, and becoming involved with un-Christlike and even immoral behavior comes from having God, the church, and our Christian friends at the center of our lives. The writer of the Book of Hebrews understood this when he warned against "forsaking the assembling of ourselves together"—an obvious reference to the importance of worship on the Lord's day (Heb. 10:25).

The Prohibition Against the Consumption of Blood

The second timeless principle in this part of our lesson comes with the repetition of the warning not to eat the blood from any sacrificed animal (17:10–16). The Leviticus writer carefully records the reason the Lord gave for this prohibition, "For the life of the flesh is in the blood . . . for it is the blood that maketh an atonement for the soul" (17:11). As the source of life, the blood belonged only to God—it was not to be violated in any way.

This, of course, points to the sacrifice of Christ on the Cross. Paul's words are familiar, ". . . we have redemption through his [Christ's] blood, even the forgiveness of sins" (Col. 1:14). The writer of 1 John worded it this way, ". . . the blood of Jesus Christ his Son cleanseth us from all sin" (1:7).

Holiness in Everyday Living (Chapters 18–20)

In these next three chapters of our Scripture lesson we move from teaching on ceremonial holiness to moral impurity and its consequences. In other words, if our worship is authentic, it will produce a life of moral integrity. Being in fellowship with God makes a difference in our sense of values and in the way we live.

Before moving ahead for a closer look at the individual paragraphs within this block of Scripture (Chapters 18–20) I suggest you stop and read it in one sitting. Especially note the introduction (18:1–5) and the solemn pronouncement the Lord makes at the beginning. Then as you move toward the close of Chapter 20, verses 22 through 26, note the conclusion or summation, climaxed by the majestic words, "And ye shall be holy unto me: for I the Lord am holy, and have severed you from other people, that ye should be mine" (20:26).

Chapter 18 in our Scripture lesson is devoted to laws governing sexual behavior. The moral degradation of ancient Near Eastern and Canaanite culture is not only attested to by the Bible but is vividly pictured on clay tablet inscriptions found in Syria and southern Turkey. The children of Israel were an island in a sea of moral pollution. It was this that made it necessary for God to spell out in detail as He has in this Scripture those practices that were acceptable and those that were not.

As we make our way through one verse after another in Chapter 18, it becomes increasingly clear that any and all sexual activities and relationships outside of marriage are forbidden. The Hebrews could under no circumstances take on the moral complexion of the surrounding culture. For this reason God spelled out in plain and simple words what was acceptable and what wasn't. If they were to be a holy people, acceptable to a holy God, there could be no compromise in their relationships.

We learn from this part of our lesson that holiness in sexual behavior is rooted in the understanding that human sexuality is created by God for the intimate bonding of a man and woman in marriage, out of which comes the creation of new life. Any variation from this standard is unacceptable.

We, too, as Christians are called to be islands of moral integrity in a world with shaded moral standards. The temptations to ease the standards are strong, but the call to sexual holiness as spelled out in our lesson is as valid for our day as it was for ancient Israel. As people of God, we are called to be holy in our sexual behavior. It is by our example that people will be convinced of the value of a holy lifestyle.

As we move into Chapter 19, we encounter a concise summary of the Law with a strong emphasis on

Holiness in Sexual Behavior

Spiritual and Social Rules

the holiness of God in His relationship with His people (19:1–4). Three commandments in particular are singled out for special emphasis: reverence for parents, the keeping of the Sabbath, and the prohibition of idol worship of any kind.

When we look closely at this particular section of Scripture, we need to be reminded that the Hebrews were living as nomads in the wilderness of the Sinai Peninsula in the midst of rough and brutal tribes who practiced child-burning, copulation with animals, gross cruelty in war and peace, cruel treatment of slaves and animals, and abuse of women. Throughout this entire section of Scripture we find a constant repetition of the words, "The Lord said unto Moses." This underlines the truth that it is God who is speaking. These aren't human theories on relationships; they are *the Word of God*. It is important, too, that we understand these commandments were not given to restrict but to liberate the Hebrews to be the people of God.

You will notice that the fifth commandment given to Moses on Mount Sinai is mentioned first (19:3a). This suggests that the honoring of parents is of vital importance to the life of the community. Both father and mother were to be trusted and revered. This attitude was the foundation of Hebrew family life, and it stood out in stark contrast to the chaos in human relationships characteristic of the pagan tribes who were neighbors of the children of Israel. The stability of home and family life was essential to holiness for the Hebrews then even as it is for us today. Society is only as strong as our family relationships.

The second commandment underlined here is "keep my sabbaths" (19:3b). The Sabbath or the Lord's day was not a human invention but a gift from God to all of His people. Unfortunately, this is a commandment that is taken all too lightly in our twentieth-century culture. Perhaps this is an overreaction to a rigidity that made Sunday for many a day of dread rather than worship. But I sometimes wonder if the pendulum hasn't swung too far the other way with our "anything goes" approach to the Lord's Day. I believe as members of the family of God, we are called to be holy in our observance of His day.

The third commandment the Leviticus writer focuses on here is the prohibition against idol worship—the worship of false gods (19:4). Only the Hebrews worshiped the true God, the Creator of the universe. They were surrounded by neighbors involved in the grossest forms of pagan worship. God wanted them to understand there could be no compromise in their complete allegiance to Him. He was not just a God among gods; He was the only God! The point is driven home again, "I am the Lord your God."

This third prohibition has powerful implications for us in spite of the fact that we may not be guilty of making "molten gods." Our idolatry occurs whenever we put anything or anyone on the same or higher level as God in our lives. Trusting in wealth or marriage or career or our country more than God is idolatry.

Recently a woman and her teenage daughter sat in my office and unraveled a tale all too familiar in American life today. Just two years before they had moved into their dream home—the result of years of working, planning, and saving. A year later a condo in the mountains was added, and the "good life" began in earnest. The care and the enjoyment of these two homes absorbed all of their time and resources, but life was exhilirating. Everything seemed to be going well until, without prior hint or notice, the husband and father announced that he was moving out to start life over with someone else.

"Now I see," the woman said with heartbreak in her voice, "that I put my faith in the false gods of property and wealth, truly believing that in them we would find our security and happiness." From the time of ancient Israel right up to the high tech world of the late-twentieth century, worship of false gods of any form has brought nothing but anguish to people.

Sharing and Caring

Next, our Leviticus writer once again turns our attention to the peace or shared offering (19:5–10). You recall that we've already studied the rules for making the peace offering (3:1–17; 7:11–38), but in mentioning it again now special emphasis is put upon the voluntary nature of the offering and the fact that the meat from the sacrifice is to be eaten without undue delay. This is followed in verses 9 and 10 by the code that required a farmer to leave what later Jewish writers called "the sixteenth" of the harvest for the poor.

Here we have a delightful and most important emphasis on the necessity to care for and share with the poor and the hungry in our work and worship. You will recall that the peace or shared offering was to be celebrated with one's friends. It was a time of sharing and of community fellowship. And the rule laid down in verses 9 and 10 became very much a part of Israel's economical and religious life. This is beautifully illustrated in the marvelous story of Ruth, the poor widow, who gathered grain for food from around the edges of the field owned by Boaz, who later became her husband.

This should not be an outdated concept but is meant to be an integral part of Christian work and worship today. Newspaper and television reporters frequently highlight the condition of starving people in certain of the Third World countries. It is painfully easy to ignore them, but these are our Christian responsibilities. At the same time, though, we are equally responsible for the hungry and the destitute in our own communities.

In the town where I live a Christian layman purchased a large home and hired a couple to supervise a shelter for families in temporary need of housing. Surrounding churches in the community are responsible for providing an evening meal for anyone who is there. But instead of just giving the food, those who provide it are required to join with their less fortunate friends in enjoying the meal and in the evening worship time that follows.

Everyone I know who has cared and shared as a part of this ministry has expressed appreciation for the opportunity to witness to his or her faith in this way. In fact, we have a waiting list of church folk who want to be involved. We are learning the truth of the words of Jesus as quoted by Paul, "It is more blessed to give than to receive" (Acts 20:35).

Loving One's Neighbor

In continuing this very practical section on personal holiness, our Leviticus writer now directs our attention to the eighth, ninth, and third commandments in that order. Honesty in our dealing both with the affluent and the poor is God's basic standard for our conduct. Stealing, fraud, lying, and swearing falsely against another are all interrelated and prohibited.

Being dishonest with our fellow human beings can take a variety of forms: sexual harrassment in the marketplace, the slow payment of wages or bills due, taking unfair advantage of an employee (19:11–13).

Next follows the prohibition against taking unfair advantage of and being cruel to those with the physical handicaps of blindness and deafness. From this we see that our rather recent concern for the handicapped has its roots in ancient biblical history. We are now alert to providing special parking places for the handicapped, to building special ramps for wheelchair access to sidewalks and buildings, and to offering expanding sanitary facilities for the physically impaired. These are all ways for our twentieth-century obedience to some very practical rules of behavior.

Then follows the great climax to this section, as we are admonished not to hate our neighbors but to love them, "Thou shalt love thy neighbor as thyself" (19:18b). You will remember that Jesus quoted this in His Sermon on the Mount (Matt. 5:43), in His conversation with the rich young ruler (Matt. 19:19), and in connection with the parable of the good Samaritan (Luke 10:27). In addition, Jesus also referred to it as the "second" commandment in his response to the lawyer's question, "Which is the greatest commandment?" (Matt. 22:36–39).

When Jesus quoted that portion of Leviticus 19:18 in the Sermon on the Mount, He said, "Ye have heard that it hath been said, Thou shalt love thy neighbor, and hate thine enemy" (Matt. 5:43). Since there is no mention in Leviticus 19:18 of hating one's enemy, we obviously have to ask, "Where did that addition come from?" We don't know for sure, but it is obvious that by Jesus' time it was commonly quoted that way. You notice Jesus didn't say, "It is written." Instead He said, "Ye have heard it said . . ." We can only assume that this is just another instance highlighting how truth can be distorted by the addition of a phrase or misquotation. But for all time Jesus made it clear that we are to *love our neighbors and our enemies* (Matt. 5:43–48).

Then, too, I think it is important for us to understand that when our writer tells us to love our neighbors *as ourselves,* the suggestion isn't some sort of narcissistic or unhealthy emotion involving an excessive preoccupation with ourselves. Rather, it is a mandate to self-giving love. It really translates into what we know as the Golden Rule, expressed by Jesus in these words, "Therefore all things whatsoever ye would that men should do to you, do ye even so to them" (Matt. 7:12).

My friend Harold has struggled all of his life with low self-esteem. For some reason, he finds it hard to love himself, but he has discovered the great joy of giving himself in service to others. In talking about this recently, he said, "It's a crazy thing, but sometimes when I'm feeling the most worthless, I find a way to help someone who's down, and I'm helped in helping them."

I'm convinced that God has built into each of us the need and the capacity to respond to others with self-giving love. I also believe that we are to offer this love to people we may at times regard as our enemies—whether they live next door or across the world.

An Assortment of Apparent Trivia and the Practical

The remainder of Chapter 19—verses 19 through 37—gives us a wide assortment of rules for living. Different teachers assign a variety of titles to these verses—"Miscellaneous Regulations," "Principles of Neighborliness," "A Practical Handbook." To twentieth-century Christians some of these rules might seem more at home in a game of Trivial Pursuit, while others still have a very practical application to us.

The transition from loving our neighbor (verse 18) to not letting cattle "gender with a diverse kind" (verse 19) seems almost ludicrous. From our viewpoint, the same can be said for not sowing "thy field with mingled seed" and not wearing "a garment mingled of linen and woolen." But we do well to remember that as unimportant as such rules seem to us, they were at least of symbolic importance to the ancient Hebrews and were given by God for a specific purpose. Holiness meant purity and separateness, and these regulations were expressions of practical holiness. In all of this, too, we confront an important truth—God is vitally concerned with every detail of our lives. Nothing that concerns us is unimportant to Him.

Next, in verses 20–22 the subject of adultery is raised again—this time as it applies to a free man and a slave woman who are engaged to be married. It is true there are certain aspects to the provisions here that are strange to us. But the underlying truth is highlighted again—sexual relationships outside of the marriage covenant were not condoned, then or now.

In verses 23 through 25, the law of the fruit trees is laid down in anticipation of that time when the Hebrews would settle in Canaan and plant their orchards. The fruit from the trees was not to be considered fit to eat during the first three years after planting. It was to be thought of as not consecrated to God—"uncircumcised"—because it had not reached its full potential. But by the fourth year the fruit would be mature and ready to be offered to the Lord. And by the fifth year the people could eat the fruit with God's blessing. For us, the fundamental principle is that everything we are and have belongs to God.

The remainder of this chapter, verses 26 through

37 give us an assorted list of rules—some of which do not have a particular application to our lives while others of them have a very up-to-date sound:

- No blood was to be consumed (19:26).
- Avoid anything associated with the occult (19:26).
- Avoid pagan acts of mourning involving disfigurement (19:27–28).
- Refuse to offer daughters as temple prostitutes (19:29).
- Observe the laws of the Sabbath (19:30).
- Do not attempt to make contact with the dead (19:31).
- Respect the aged (19:32).
- Treat foreigners with kindness and respect (19:33–34).
- Insure justice and fairness in dealings with others, especially with regard to weights and measures (19:35–36).

While certain of these rules aren't necessarily applicable to us because of the vast changes that have occurred across the centuries, there is a central and underlying principle woven through them that is timeless: Love for God and love for our neighbors wherever they are in the world is to be the governing principle in all of our relationships and activities. Nothing that has occurred in three thousand years of human history has revoked that Law!

The Penalties for Disobedience

This closing section (Chapter 20) of the discussion on holiness for everyday living will seem incredibly harsh as the penalties are spelled out for breaking the laws listed in Chapters 18, 19, and 20. Here death is ruled the penalty for sacrificing children to the pagan god Molech (20:2–5), for those involved in witchcraft (20:6), for cursing (reviling) one's parents (20:9), for sexual sins of adultery and incest (20:10–12, 17–21), for homosexuality and bestiality (20:13, 15–16). Other less heinous sins received lesser penalties.

It is quite impossible for us in any way to identify

Referred to as the Plain of Rest, this is the traditional site of the Israelite encampment at the foot of Mount Sinai.

with the setting in which the ancient Hebrews found themselves in the Sinai wilderness and later in Canaan. For over four hundred years they had lived as aliens in a foreign land, and during the last of those years had suffered severe repression in Egypt's pagan culture. But as the chosen people of God they were freed from slavery and released into the Sinai wilderness surrounded by a cruelly pagan society. Then later as they moved into Canaan their neighbors were involved in pagan practices of the most sordid kind imaginable.

God had made it plain, though, that He expected the Hebrews to live as His special people. His laws of holiness were not to be violated, and from our vantage point in history we can only wrestle with the thrust of these verses in view of God's special instructions to them, "Ye shall therefore keep all my statutes, and all my judgments, and do them: that the land, whither I bring you to dwell therein, spue [spew] you not out. And ye shall not walk in the manners of [live like] the nation, which I cast out before you [I am driving out ahead of you]: for they committed [practiced] all these things, and therefore I abhorred them. But I have said unto you, Ye shall inherit their land, and I will give it unto you to possess it, a land that floweth with milk and honey: I am the Lord your God, *which have separated you from other people*'' (20:22–24, italics mine).

Then to further underscore their identity as God's special people, He says, "And ye shall be holy unto me: for I the Lord am holy, and have severed you from other people, that ye should be mine" (20:26). As "severed" or set-apart people, there could be no participation in the foul pagan practices of their neighbors. Any violation of these instructions called for the severest of penalties. Only in this way could the ancient Hebrews understand the gravity of disobeying God's rules for their conduct.

But, unfortunately, as the pages of history flip by, we discover that even severe penalties did not at all times prevent people from breaking God's laws. And so centuries later God's ultimate plan emerged on the world scene in the person of Jesus Christ. The great Apostle to the gentiles expressed it this way in writing to the Christians in Rome, "For what the law could not do, in that it was weak through the flesh, God sending his own Son in the likeness of sinful flesh, and for sin, condemned sin in the flesh: That the righteousness of the law might be fulfilled in us, who walk not after the flesh, but after the Spirit" (Rom. 8:3–4).

The message for us in this part of our lesson is very up-to-date and clear. While we live in and are a part of our twentieth-century culture, we dare not take on the sinful ways of our neighbors who ignore the Christian message. We, too, in Christ, are a "severed" or set-apart people whose ears are "tuned to a different drummer."

Rules for the Priests (Chapters 21–22)

Until now, the Leviticus writer has focused on the holiness required of everyday folks. But in these two chapters holiness rules are spelled out for the priest. Being a priest in ancient Israel was a high and special calling. A man didn't choose to be a priest. Rather, he was chosen by God. And being a priest involved special responsibilities, for, in the deepest sense, he was the person who represented God to the people and who, in turn, represented the people before God.

In reading the rules found here, I am reminded of the attitude of some of my seminary students. As a pastor who also teaches pastors-to-be, I frequently hear a protest over the so-called double standard imposed upon us. "Why should we be expected to live up to higher standards than they?" My answer to such a question is deeply rooted in this ancient tradition.

Rules Governing Relationships

According to the rules laid down here in Chapter 21:1–6 a priest could not mourn in the usual fashion for one of his friends. In the Hebrew culture, contact with a dead body made a person ceremonially unclean. While there were not moral implications to this, a ceremonially unclean priest could not perform the normal tasks of his assignment.

Also, these verses give specific rules on the kind of a woman a priest could marry. Now, while the particular prohibitions expressed here for those early Hebrew priests don't have specific application to us today, the basic concepts hold true. All of us, ordained ministers and lay persons alike, are to live in such a way that all of our relationships are Christ-centered. If we are to be effective witnesses of Christ, our pattern of life in relationship with other people must be above reproach.

Rules Related to Effective Service

In the verses that follow in this part of our Scripture lesson (21:16–23), we learn that a priest could not perform his duties if he had physical blemishes or defects. This seems strange to us today, but for me, the symbolism of a defective person implied here is important. Defects of character in both clergy and lay persons alike stand in the way of effective service and witness.

Next, the priests were to revere the things of God

and to carry out their sacrificial rituals with care and in a manner that was honoring to the Lord (Chapter 22). Here, too, those who have been called by God and set apart as ministers of the gospel are to carry out their duties at all times in a way that is pleasing to God. However, in all of these things we need to be reminded again that in a very real sense the attitude and life-style of the Christian layperson is not intended to differ from the day-to-day thoughts and actions of an ordained clergy person. Remember, in Christ each of us is called to be a priest. Peter made this clear when he wrote, "Ye are a chosen generation, a royal priesthood" (1 Peter 2:9).

**Special Times for
Worship
(Chapters 23–26)**

God has a marvelous way of understanding the needs of His people and providing patterns that will help us in our pilgrimage of faith. Up to this point the Leviticus writer carefully gave his readers the regulations and rules for ceremonial and moral holiness. Now, in this section we are given a structure for worship—the means and rhythms for keeping in tune with God and His teachings. Here we find the provisions for the Sabbath and the special celebrations and festivals that were to be carefully observed by the Hebrews.

Across the centuries the Christian churches have developed a similar pattern—the church or liturgical year. Millions of Christians across the world begin the Christian year with Advent, starting four Sundays before Christmas. Then follows Christmas, Epiphany, Lent, Holy Week, Easter, and Pentecost. It is true, of course, that the different Christian traditions may vary the times and the emphasis, but most share a similar cycle.

In this part of our Scripture lesson we are given the basic cycle around which the worship of the Hebrew community was to revolve. The cycle is built around the number seven. The weekly Sabbath was the seventh day. The Feasts of Unleavened Bread and Tabernacles were seven days in length. On the fourteenth day (two sevens) of the first month of the worship year was celebrated the Feast of Passover, followed by the Feast of Unleavened Bread. Seven weeks later came Pentecost, also called the Feast of First Fruits or the Feast of Weeks. In the seventh month, the sacred month, three seasons of "holy convocation" occurred—on the first day, the Feast of Trumpets, on the tenth, the Day of Atonement, and on the fifteenth began the Feast of Tabernacles which continued for seven days. The seventh year was observed as a Year of Sabbath—a year of rest for the land, and after seven sevens of years came the culmination of the entire cycle in the great Year of Jubilee.

All of the sacred seasons are designated as "holy convocations," the first of which was the weekly observance of the Sabbath (23:1–3). Its distinctiveness was that no work was to be done. Along with the Day of Atonement, these were the only days on which all work was forbidden. We have already seen the importance of the Sabbath, both for rest and for worship. And we have learned that the Sabbath was to be a day of joy and gladness, celebrating the goodness and love of God.

The Sabbath

The first feast of the worship year was Passover, followed immediately by the Feast of Unleavened Bread for one week (23:4–14). Our celebration of Easter is rooted in these feasts, for it was on the Passover that Jesus became the sacrificial Lamb of God. The Passover, of course, was the central feast in their liturgical year, because it was the time of their remembering and celebrating their deliverance by God from slavery in Egypt.

The Passover and Feast of Unleavened Bread

The central feature of the Feast of Unleavened Bread was the exclusion of leaven or yeast from the ancient Hebrews' food for the entire week. In fact, they developed elaborate rituals to cleanse their house of any fragments of leaven during that time. It was this tradition that prompted Paul to use the image of yeast in his instructions to the Christians in Corinth with these words, "Purge out therefore the old leaven, that ye may be a new lump, as ye are unleavened. For even Christ our passover is sacrificed for us: Therefore let us keep the feast, not with old leaven, neither with the leaven of malice and wickedness; but with the unleavened bread of sincerity and truth" (1 Cor. 5:7–8).

Another feature of this feast was that of the offering of the firstfruits of the spring harvest. This, obviously, symbolized their recognition that the best of everything belonged to God. Paul applied the firstfruit concept to the resurrection of Jesus, "But now is Christ risen from the dead, and become the firstfruits of them that slept" (1 Cor. 15:20).

Both the Passover and the Feast of Unleavened Bread are closely tied to our understanding of the meaning of Christ's death and resurrection.

The Feast of Pentecost

Seven weeks following the Passover and Unleavened Bread Feasts, on the fiftieth day, came Pentecost (a Greek word meaning fiftieth) (23:15–22). This was a harvest festival in early June. As the firstfruits marked the beginning of the barley harvest, so Pentecost marked the conclusion of the wheat harvest. It is significant that this celebration was accompanied by a reminder to provide for the poor by leaving the corners and the gleanings for them.

It was on the Day of Pentecost that the Holy Spirit was poured out upon the believers in Jerusalem in a special way (Acts 1–2), making Pentecost the day when we celebrate what might be called the birthday of the church.

The Feast of Trumpets

As the seventh day was holy, so the seventh month was regarded as a holy month. The Jewish seventh month would be the equivalent of our October, during which there were three celebrations (23:23–25). On the first day of this sacred month was a special "holy convocation" marked by the sounding of trumpets. This set off the sacred month as a month of joy. A delightful description of a very special Feast of Trumpets is found in Nehemiah 8:9–12 when the exiles had returned to Jerusalem. I suggest you stop a moment and read those four verses.

The Day of Atonement

We have already learned about the Day of Atonement in Leviticus 16. This was, indeed, the great day of the entire worship year and was held on the tenth day of the sacred month (23:26–32). This was a time of national repentance and forgiveness, and it was on this day that the scapegoat, bearing the sins of the people, was driven out into the wilderness.

The Feast of Tabernacles

The Feast of Tabernacles was a unique festival lasting a week beginning with the fifteenth day of the seventh month (23:33–44). It was undoubtedly the most celebrative time of all, for the people left their houses and clustered in temporary shelters made of branches of trees. We would call this a community camp-out.

Living in the shelters was to be a perpetual reminder to the Hebrews that they had once lived under such temporary conditions when they had first been delivered from Egypt. This feast also marked the end of the agricultural year and was the time for a party in which God's goodness and faithfulness was celebrated.

Holy Light and Holy Bread

Next comes a brief insertion giving the specifics regarding the oil for the lamps of the Golden Candlestick and the bread to be placed on the Table in the Holy Place of the Tabernacle (24:1–9). Other details concerning these items of Tabernacle furniture were given earlier, but included here are certain details not mentioned before. In reading these verses we are reminded that the symbolism of the light and the bread is still central to our experience of Jesus as the Light of the world and the Bread of life.

Tragic Blasphemy

The Leviticus writer also includes at this point the tragic story of a man who rebelled against God and apparently tried to influence others to join him (24:10–23). Here we learn the true meaning of "taking God's name in vain," in violation of the Commandment. This was no mere matter of casual and careless speech, but an act of outright rebellion against God. As you can see in reading this story, the penalty was severe, but so was the violation.

Here we have what is known as the *lex talionis* principle—"eye for eye, tooth for tooth" (24:20). And while this seems to be a severe form of retaliation, it was actually a mercy move away from the custom at the time when the loss of one tooth by a person called for retaliation resulting in the loss of all the other person's teeth. But we must always read this Leviticus verse in the light of Jesus' words centuries later, "Ye have heard that it hath been said, An eye for an eye and a tooth for a tooth: but I say unto you, That ye resist not evil: but whosoever shall smite thee on thy right cheek, turn to him the other also" (Matt. 5:38–39).

The Sabbath Year

The sacred observances for the Hebrews included not only the seventh day and the seventh month but also the seventh year (25:1–7). This observance would become effective when they were settled in the land of Canaan. The Sabbath year was a special time in which the land was allowed to rest and be renewed—as in crop rotation. It was a time of celebration for the goodness and faithfulness of God.

The Year of Jubilee

No celebration or observance could have made a more dramatic statement about their belief that the land and their possessions belonged to God than the Year of Jubilee (25:8–55). This observance was a radical and social economic idea—the supreme climax of all the sacred seasons and festivals. The Leviticus writer tells us that every fiftieth year, beginning on the Day of Atonement, the trumpets were to sound throughout all the land to announce the beginning of this special time.

The identifying slogan for this year of celebration was, "Proclaim liberty throughout all the land unto all the inhabitants thereof" (25:10). During this year property was to be returned to its original owners under fair conditions, slaves were to be set free, interest-free loans were to be made to the poor—it was a year designed to give every person a new and fresh start.

The Jubilee Year prevented the accumulation of wealth by a very few. For example, if a man had lost his inherited land and his freedom because of an inability to pay his debts, these were all recovered during the Jubilee Year. It was a time of redistribution without excessive control or injustice.

The Jubilee Year was a test of faith in the promises of God. We read here that peace and blessing are promised to all who keep the Jubilee. But it took faith to neither sow nor reap on the fiftieth year—faith that God would provide. Actually, though, we don't have much evidence that this celebration was put into consistent practice. It appears to be more an ideal that was not realized than a regular part of Israel's life.

But then we have to ask, "Should the ideal be abandoned?" Never! Luke tells us (Luke 4:16–19) that at the beginning of His public ministry Jesus quotes these words from the prophet Isaiah: "The Spirit of the Lord God is upon me; because the Lord hath anointed me to preach good tidings unto the meek; he hath sent me to bind up the brokenhearted, to proclaim liberty to the captives, and the opening of the prison to them that are bound; To proclaim the acceptable year of the Lord" (Isa. 61:1–2a).

This was the language of the Year of Jubilee, and it is the language of Jesus' new society today—His kingdom *now* that will be made perfect when He comes again.

The Blessing and the Curse

Throughout our study of this lesson we have taken a close look at what is commonly referred to by Bible students as "The Holiness Code"—God's pattern for the forms and times of Israel's worship. As followers and worshipers of a holy God, the people of Israel were to be a holy people. In their daily life-style and in their worship, they were to be a set-apart people—distinctly different from their pagan neighbors. And so the Leviticus writer has been careful to spell out God's direct word to His people as to the kind of behavior that was agreeable and acceptable to Him.

Now, in the style of ancient Near Eastern treaties or agreements we come to a concluding section (Chapter 26) which contains blessings—promises—for those who obey the instructions and the terms offered, and curses—threats, warnings—on those who do not. After reading Leviticus 26, I suggest you take a few moments and also read Exodus 23:25–33, Deuteronomy 28:1–68, and Joshua 24:19–20. The similarity will be apparent in all of these.

There was no question in the minds of the ancient Hebrews that obedience to God would result in His blessing, and disobedience would insure God's curse—His judgment. And now, I'm sure, they were delighted to hear God's promise of blessing as the reward for their obedience (26:3–13). At the same time they must have shuddered as they read the curses—judgment—that would be their reward for disobedience (26:14–39).

But all of this is followed by the marvelously affirming word of God's unfailing grace as He assures them that whatever happens He will remember His covenant with the Patriarchs (26:42). Then come the reassuring words, "I will not cast them [the Hebrew people] away, neither will I abhor them, to destroy them utterly, and to break my covenant with them: for I am the Lord their God. But I will for their sakes remember the covenant of their ancestors, whom I brought forth out of the land of Egypt in the sight of the heathen, that I might be their God: I am the Lord" (26:44–45).

A study of this chapter should not incite us to obedience merely to gain rewards and blessings, or to avoid punishment. We can rest in the confidence that God's grace is sufficient for all our sins. But we know, too, that we must never presume on His mercy and grace as though obedience to His Word is unimportant, or disobedience is without its consequences.

As Christians our hope is fixed firmly in the truth of Paul's words to his friends in Rome, "There is therefore now no condemnation to them which are in Christ Jesus, who walk not after the flesh, but after the Spirit. For the law of the Spirit of life in Christ Jesus hath made me free from the law of sin and death" (Rom. 8:1–2).

Vows and Tithes (Chapter 27)

This closing chapter of our Leviticus study discusses "vows" and "tithes." Vows were commitments which placed a person or property in a special relationship to God that was not required by the Law. It is emphasized in these closing verses that true holiness is much more than just keeping the rules of life and worship. Rather, holiness involves a total commitment of oneself to the service of God. It is a matter of offering all that we are and have and hope to be to God in worship. Vows could involve the dedication of persons (27:1–8), the dedication of animals (27:9–13), and the dedication of a person's houses and fields (27:14–25).

In making these vows, a person was offering God something more than what was required by Law. Those offerings required by the Law were God's already. For example, the tithe was not something that could be vowed—it already belonged to the Lord. To withhold the tithe was considered a crime against God (Mal. 3:8).

While the New Testament doesn't directly specify the tithe as a requirement, it certainly establishes the principle of proportionate giving as a normal expression of our Christian commitment (1 Cor. 16:2; 2 Cor. 8–9). Anything less than the time-honored principle of the tithe, even though it may no longer be binding, certainly seems a minimal standard in the spirit of New Testament freedom.

Epilogue

With the conclusion of this lesson we have completed our very brief study or overview of the Book of Leviticus. Hopefully, we've come to a new appreciation of what, I'm sure, has been an obscure and virtually unknown part of the Bible.

Together, we have discovered that the central theme of what God said to Moses so long ago was not for ancient Israel alone, but is for us as well. Holiness—the full consecration of our whole selves to God—is the reason for our very existence. And this is made possible through Jesus Christ, our great High Priest, who was the final and complete sacrifice for our sin. Through Christ's love and by the power of the Holy Spirit alive in us, we can, by His grace, be holy!

Lord, I give You my life anew today. I commit every moment to You and Your purposes. Let my entire life today be glorifying to You. AMEN.

WHAT THIS SCRIPTURE MEANS TO ME
Leviticus 17—27

After my first week of college, when the thrill of being on my own in a new place had worn off, I found myself alone at my desk one Sunday afternoon. Scattered in front of me were the papers and booklets I'd collected during the week.

First I read over a booklet of campus regulations—speed limits, library hours, parking restrictions, etc. Then I thumbed through the list of dorm rules—cafeteria hours, meal tickets, rules on having guests, curfews, even how to empty trash. After that I glanced at a notebook of the sorority's code—penalties for lateness, for not attending meetings, for wearing jeans to class, for not attending functions, and so on.

On top of that were detailed instructions for every class. My eyes swam as I looked over the typed sheets of assignments and deadlines.

I was miserably overwhelmed. How could I ever integrate all these rules into my day-to-day life? I was ready to give up and go home.

This past week as I was reading our lesson, I tried to visualize the Israelites in the desert after their dramatic escape from the Egyptians. As they camped at the foot of Mount Sinai, waiting for Moses to return, they became bored and impatient. They wanted a splashy, spectacular God they could see and worship, like the golden calf they had built. So how did they feel when Moses came down with nothing but a lot of rules?

Today we have the benefit of looking at the Israelites through the lens of later events. But in order truly to know and understand how they felt, we need to zip back in time. We need to try to put ourselves in their sandals.

The Israelites had been slaves as a people for four hundred years. They had no laws spelling out right and wrong. Once the excitement of their escape was over, day-to-day life in the desert probably felt very uncertain. The people lived in temporary tents; they had no maps to the Promised Land. They were hungry, dirty, and crowded by griping, homesick neighbors.

In these circumstances, God needed to lay down acceptable rules of behavior. Like college freshmen, the Israelites found themselves with a new freedom, in close living quarters with others. One reason God gave the Israelites dietary, social, marriage, sexual, and worship laws was to prevent chaos. He wanted to keep them from killing each other, spreading disease, and breaking vows.

Giving the Law was one of God's ways of showing love to the Israelites. They needed to learn how to live and grow and mature as the people of God. The Law gave them guidelines in how to live with each other. It also showed them how to purify themselves before God in order to keep their end of the Covenant as His children. If they followed the Law, they would be in a right relationship with God.

Several centuries later, Jesus entered human history. Because of His life, death, and resurrection, our being right with God does not depend on outward actions, but on acceptance of Jesus as Savior and Lord. Jesus summed up and lived out the essence of the Law: Love God, and love your neighbor.

For me, this means I am saved by Jesus' action, not my own. However, it doesn't mean that my actions aren't important. Regular worship, good citizenship, and responsibility to my family do not determine my salvation. But because I have been saved by Christ, He gives me the power and the strength and the desire to keep the rules I need to keep.

LESSON 3
Numbers 1–10:10

Preparing for the Journey

Lord God, May Your Word be a source of strength and help for me, especially when I must journey into the wilderness of the unknown and the uncertain. Amen.

The Book of Numbers may rank alongside Leviticus as another of the lesser-known and used books of the Bible. Those not familiar with this book are indeed the poorer for their lack. I must confess to you that I have come to know and love Leviticus and Numbers in a new way in recent years. I only wish I had discovered them sooner.

The name "Numbers" makes the book sound more like a telephone directory than the great drama it is. This name apparently grew out of the lists that appear in the narrative, though they are not of extreme importance. The Hebrew title for the book is "In The Wilderness" from the opening words (1:1)—a much more accurate title.

An Ongoing Story

As Leviticus is continuous with the narrative begun in Exodus, so Numbers continues the Leviticus story. The Hebrew people have been delivered from their bondage in Egypt. They are now camped on the Sinai peninsula, east of Egypt.

Let's review briefly the sequence of events. In Exodus 25–40, Moses was given instructions for the building of the Tabernacle (their portable center of worship); in Leviticus 1–16, Moses was given the instruction for the sacrifices, the priesthood, and the Day of Atonement; and in Leviticus 17–27, the Hebrews received the Code for Holiness—the proper life-style growing out of their worship.

In the opening chapters of Numbers, God gives Moses instructions for preparing the people to move out from the Sinai wilderness, north to Canaan, the land promised to Abraham and his descendants. In the second section of Numbers, Israel is on the journey through the wilderness, a long and frustrating sojourn of almost forty years. In the third portion, covering about five months, Israel has arrived at their point of entrance into Canaan.

I'm sure we all would like to know more of the details about Israel's life in the desert. But it is impossible to reconstruct those details with accuracy because the Numbers writer was preoccupied with what was going on between God and the people. His purpose in writing was not to give us a detailed history of their journeys and life-style.

This is why some scholars have suggested that Numbers is not unlike the literature of Greek drama. The keen ethical focus and the high spiritual drama put this in the genre of classical tragedy. Moses, the central human figure of the drama, is portrayed with friends and foes: Aaron and Miriam; Joshua and Hobab; Korah, Dathan, and Abiram; Balak and Balaam.

As the story progresses, we see Moses stretched to the breaking point; he cries out in desperation to God. In a moment of pride, he falls into sin. The people Moses is leading are forever complaining, whining, and demanding the impossible. Then there are the tabernacle, the cloud by day, the fire by night, the perpetual smoke of the sacrifices, the wars, the stress of the arduous journey in the desert, the hope of the Promised Land—all of these add up to a powerful drama perhaps unparalleled in human history.

The Focus of the Drama

The central focus of the drama is upon God's purpose for His people, and the disclosure of His steadfast and unfailing love for them. In the midst of every scene stands the towering figure of Moses, spokesman for God, faithful though imperfect, admired and adored one day and targeted for abuse and derision the next. But through it all he never loses his faith in the God of Abraham, Isaac, and Jacob, the God whose mercy and severity are like two sides of a coin.

We would be less than honest if we entered this drama without the troubling recognition that it breathes a militaristic spirit. Israel cannot move into Canaan except by military conquest. There is no thought of loving enemies.

When the signal is finally given, the entire Hebrew army will move across the Jordan River to conquer the land God had promised their forefathers. Even the men of Reuben, Gad, and the half-tribe of Manasseh who had been assigned land on the east side of the Jordan would leave their families behind and march beside their brothers until the occupation was complete. For them, the pattern of war was justified by their mission and destiny.

The events of our lesson (1:1–10:10) cover a period of only twenty days, from the first day of the second month (1:1) to the twentieth day of the second month (10:11). Since the Exodus and the encampment at Mount Sinai, the Hebrews had been a gathered community, listening as God gave them instructions for worship and living through Moses. Now begins a grouping and organizing in preparation for moving out toward the Promised Land.

After the first census (Ch. 1), the basic order and organization of their march was established (Ch. 2). In Chapters 3, 4, and 8, the Levites are organized so they can effectively care for the Tabernacle. In Chapters 5 and 6 the purity and holiness of the camp is provided for and insured. And in Chapter 7, one of the longest chapters in the Bible, we have the careful and almost tedious listing of the offering brought by each of the twelve tribal leaders to provide for the Tabernacle worship when the camp is on the move. Then, when all of the preparations are completed, two special trumpets made "of beaten silver" will sound the call for all of the people to assemble in readiness to begin the long and difficult journey (10:1).

We have here a story, not of a people clustered around a shrine at Mount Sinai with tablets of stone containing God's Law in a box. Rather, we have a drama enacted by a people who are called to move out and become the channel of God's redemptive love for all humankind. The movement is about to begin in which "all of the families of the earth shall be blessed" (Gen. 12:3).

The First Census (Chapter 1)

For more than a year the Hebrews had been camped near Mount Sinai (since Exod. 19:1). Now, their first step before breaking camp was organizational—God told Moses to count the people. This meant their period of waiting was about over.

In the ancient world there were two occasions for a census—one was for taxation, and the other was for military purposes. And since the phrase "able to go forth to war" is repeated fourteen times in this chapter, it is pretty obvious that the reason for this head count had to do with an assessment of their military strength.

Names of the Tribal Leaders

The Numbers writer next moves on to give us the names of the Hebrew tribal leaders (1:5–19). It is quite significant, I believe, that as we run down this list of twenty-four names (twelve men and their fathers), nine of them include the name for God—El: *El*izur, my God is a Rock; Shelumi*el,* God is my Peace; Nethane*el,* God gives; *El*iab, my God is a Father; *El*ishama, my God listens; Gamali*el,* God is my Reward; Pagi*el,* God is my Fortune; *El*iasaph, my God adds; Deu*el* (probably Reu*el*), God is a Friend. You will recall that to the ancients, the naming of a child had almost mystical significance. Names were chosen either related to the experience in having the child or to some intuition about their personality or character or to some hope for their future.

One name that does not include the name of God but that is noteworthy is Nahshon, son of Amminadab (1:7). His name is found in the genealogy of David as given in Ruth 4:20. It is also found in the genealogies of Jesus (Matt. 1:4 and Luke 4:32–33). Here was a man who would spend most of his life as a warrior in the wilderness, yet he is very much a part of God's redemptive plan in the coming of the Messiah centuries later.

Virtually nothing more is known about Nahshon, this ancient prince of Judah; he is an unknown. Yet he becomes a vital link in the fulfillment of God's purposes, and is an object lesson for us as we realize that every life is a purposeful part of all that God is doing. What a marvelous idea—through us, even now, the drama of divine redemption is slowly but steadily unfolding.

I remember so well a young man who, just a short time after he had made his Christian commitment, became a part of a Bible study group in which I was involved. During the course of our discussions he told us about his struggle with a very negative self-image. From his earliest childhood his parents had let him know that he hadn't been wanted and was not loved. He went on to tell us about the help he had received in psychotherapy. "But," he said, "as far as I've come, I've never experienced the kind of self-understanding and acceptance that has given me a sense of worth and confidence. But in this group I've learned that Jesus really knows and calls me by name. In fact, He has given me a new name, 'loved by God,' and that has made me into a whole new person." Through each little-known member of our group, God's plan of redemption for this young man was being worked out!

The Numbering

In verses 20 through 46 of this first chapter the number of the potential warriors is given tribe by tribe. There has long been question and speculation about the proper interpretation of the numbers listed. If we add up the totals given, it comes to

603,550 able-bodied men over twenty years old. Now, if we add to that the uncounted Levites, the women, everyone under twenty, and those not qualified to fight, the total could easily run to more than two million.

This numbering would seem to indicate a body of people much too large for the movements about to be described and doesn't seem to square with the various rolls found in the Book of Judges. Translators readily admit they don't know how to translate the Hebrew words in this section. For example, recent studies seem to indicate that the Hebrew word in this part of our lesson that is translated "thousand" might actually have been a designation for a military unit such as a modern "squad."

Bible scholars wish they had more knowledge of how to translate the figures, but God is not limited in His ability to provide for them. Of this we can be absolutely certain.

The Unnumbered Levites

In this numbering process the Lord made it clear that no member of the tribe of Levi was to be counted—none of them was eligible for military service (1:47–53). It was their specific task to care for the Tabernacle. When the camp moved, the Levites were responsible for the entire dismantling and transportation process. And then when camp was reestablished, the Levites reassembled the entire Tabernacle complex along with all of the furnishings. They were the God-selected custodians of the place of worship and were to camp around it when it was in position.

The service of the Levites and their custodianship of the Tabernacle underlines its importance as God's dwelling place among the people. This was holy ground; God was there in the middle of their camp. The image takes on an added and personal diminsion for us in the reference to Jesus in John's Gospel, "And the Word was made flesh and dwelt [tabernacled] among us" (John 1:14). In the Sinai desert, God was with His people; in the twentieth-century wilderness in which we live, in Jesus, God literally comes to dwell among us!

The Camp (Chapter 2)

When I read the Lord's instructions to Moses and Aaron and the children of Israel in this part of our Scripture lesson, I am reminded again of just how much attention our heavenly Father pays to the details of our lives. He is not a remote, far-off God who leaves us to shift for ourselves. And we are about to see a marvelous illustration of this truth as we turn our attention to God's next words to Moses (2:1).

The Arrangement

While the Hebrews didn't know it at this particular time, they would be a people on the move for the next forty years. It was God's intention that they go directly from Mount Sinai to Canaan and occupy that Land of Promise. But as we shall see, this was not to be. Instead, they would spend almost forty long years in the desert wilderness because of their disobedience.

To make certain that their movements and their camp were orderly, God now gives them a precise blueprint as to their formation on the march and in camp. The Tabernacle, the dwelling place of God, was always to be in the center. Camped immediately in protective formation around the Tabernacle were the sons of Aaron on the east side toward the rising sun; descendants of the three sons of Levi camped in formation around the other three sides of the Tabernacle—the Merarites to the north, the Gershonites to the west, and the Kohathites on the south. Then the remainder of the tribes were arranged in an orderly design with three on each side.

On the east beyond the tents of Moses and Aaron and his sons was the tribe of Judah in the center. Judah was flanked on the north by the tribe of Issachar and on the south by the tribe of Zebulun. Beyond the Merarites on the north side was the tribe of Dan in the center. To the east of Dan was the tribe of Naphtali, and the tribe of Asher was positioned to the west of Dan.

The three tribes on the west side of the Tabernacle beyond the camp of the Gershonites were Ephraim in the center with Benjamin on the north and Manasseh

on the south. And just beyond the camp of the Kohathites on the south side of the Tabernacle was the
tribe of Reuben in the center, flanked by Gad to the
west and Simeon to the east.

The four principal tribes occupied the center spot
both in camp and on the march—Judah on the east,
Dan on the north, Ephraim on the west, and Reuben
on the south. In later times each of the four principal
tribes was represented by a symbol: Judah by the
lion, the strongest and most powerful of all the animals; Reuben by a human face that expressed care
and compassion; Ephraim by an ox, expressive of
reliability and fertility; and Dan by an eagle, representing freedom and nobility.

It is interesting that early in the Christian tradition
these same four symbols became associated with the
four Gospels. Matthew came to be represented by
the face of a man; Mark by a lion; Luke by an ox; and
John by the eagle. Most certainly, a composite of
these four likenesses gives us a vivid picture of what
our lives, as the people of God, are meant to be. This
was true in the Sinai desert over three thousand years
ago, and it is equally true in the complexities of our
modern urban world.

As we read this part of our Scripture lesson, we
continue to be impressed with the Lord's attention to
detail as He focuses on the specifics related to the
duties of the priests and Levites.

The Priests and the Levites (Chapters 3–4)

As we have already seen, the tribe of Levi, of
which Moses and the priestly family of Aaron were
members (Exod. 2), was set apart by God for unique
service in the worship life of the Hebrews. As such,
they were assigned a place of honor both in camp and
on the march.

You will recall that when Aaron gave in to the will
of the people during Moses' long absence on the
mountain and made the golden bull-calf, Moses,
upon his return, called the people to a renewed
commitment. In response, it was the Levites who
immediately declared their loyalty to God (Exod.
32:26, 28).

Chosen for Service

73

Now, the Levites were chosen to assist the priests and to look after the Tabernacle in camp and on the march (3:5–10). They were to be lay assistants in the worship of the Lord. A New Testament counterpart to their activities may be seen in the selection of deacons in the first-century church (Acts 6).

The Sons of Aaron

At the very beginning of the Scripture lesson the Numbers writer refers to the sons of Aaron who were chosen to serve under him as priests—representatives of the people before God. Only two of Aaron's sons, Eleazar and Ithamar, were left to assist their father. You recall that in an earlier lesson we were told of the disobedience and rebellion of the other two sons, Nadab and Abihu. Mention of this tragedy appears five times in the books of Leviticus and Numbers as a constant reminder of the importance of maintaining purity and integrity in the worship of God.

The Levites—Consecrated for a Special Role

Two places in Chapter 3—verses 12 and 13, and verses 41 and 45—refer to the consecration of the Levites as substitutes for the Hebrew firstborn males who at the time of the first Passover in Egypt were specified as being set apart for God. You recall that on the fateful night when the tenth plague brought death to the firstborn Egyptian males the Hebrews were spared. It was then the Lord told Moses that "the firstborn . . . both of man and of beast" were to be set aside for Him (Exod. 13:2).

But now, a new provision is made. Members of the tribe of Levi are to serve in the place of the Hebrew firstborn sons. To us this may seem an unimportant detail. But as we will see shortly, it pointed to a most important part of God's plan.

Next, God instructs Moses to take a census of the tribe of Levi (3:14–39). When that count was finalized, it was discovered that the total number of Levites was just 273 short of equaling all of the Hebrew male firstborn (3:40–43). In other words, if one Levite was to be consecrated for the Lord's service in place of every Hebrew male firstborn, then 273 were without a substitute representative.

In response to this shortage, a special provision was made (3:44–51). For each of the 273 Hebrew male firstborn who were not represented by a substitute Levite, five shekels would be paid into a Tabernacle fund. They were redeemed by what came eventually to be called "redemption money." Redemption was seen as the way in which someone or something that had fallen under the control of someone else could be freed.

This simply means that in this dramatic action which dominates so much of this chapter we are able to capture something of the New Testament understanding of Jesus as our redemption. As the firstborn or only-born Son of God, He is our substitute; He is our redemption. Paul expressed this so clearly to the Christians in Corinth when he wrote, "What? know ye not that your body is the temple of the Holy Ghost which is in you, which ye have of God, and ye are not your own? For ye are bought with a price: therefore glorify God in your body, and in your spirit, which are God's" (1 Cor. 6:19–20).

A beautiful illustration of redemption through Christ and the freedom that comes with it is seen in the lives of a group of folks who meet at our church every Wednesday night. All of these people have wrestled with the problem of alcohol and are active in either AA or Alanon. Having found their "higher power" to be focused in Jesus Christ, they come together for prayer and Christian fellowship. Jane expressed it well for most of them one evening when she said, "I was *owned*—body, mind, and soul—by alcohol. I was a slave to booze. But now I have a new Owner, a gracious, loving Master who has set me free from the old bondage and given me the freedom not to drink. I've been redeemed!"

Careful detail and instructions are also spelled out in these verses covering the precise duties of each of the three families that make up the tribe of Levi. The origin of these three "families" were the sons of Levi—Gershon, Kohath, and Merari (Exod. 6:16).

The Kohathites. When the camp was being moved, the Kohathites were responsible for actually carrying

The Service of the Levite Families

"the most holy things" used in the Tabernacle, but they could only be handled after Aaron and his sons had covered them and placed them in their wrappings (3:31; 4:1–20).

The Gershonites. This family group was assigned the task of carrying all of the hangings, curtains and coverings for the Tabernacle, with the exception of the veil which was used as a covering for the Ark (3:25–26; 4:21–28).

The Merarites. The task of carrying the frames, the crossbars, posts and bases, as well as the hardware for the curtains of the courtyard was assigned to the Merarites (3:36–37; 4:29–33).

As we read this part of our Scripture lesson, we can't help but be impressed with the enormity of the task involved in the assembling and disassembling and the hauling of the Tabernacle and its furnishing when the Hebrews were moving from one campsite to another.

Absolutely nothing associated with the Tabernacle—God's dwelling place in the midst of His people—was left to chance. The Tabernacle was a holy place, and everything associated with it had to be handled according to plan.

While the structure and the rituals associated with our places of worship in the twentieth-century church are quite different from what is described in our lesson, I somehow feel the Hebrew's sense of reverence and awe associated with the house of God gives us a model we might follow more closely. Our over-casual attitude toward worship may well cause us to miss some of the deep meanings and experiences that have marked our Christian faith and church life since its beginnings in the first century.

At the same time, picking up on Paul's reference to our bodies being the temple of the Holy Spirit, we are reminded of the reverence and care we should show toward this part of God's creation.

Banned from the Camp (5:1–4)

As we have seen in our Leviticus lessons, both moral and ceremonial cleanness was considered absolutely essential in God's presence. And the Tabernacle was indeed the place of God's presence in the

A view such as the one pictured here in the Sinai peninsula was a familiar sight to the people of Israel during the year they were camped at the foot of Mount Sinai while they waited for word from the Lord to move toward Canaan.

camp. So, in these four verses instructions are now given for those who were considered "unclean"— victims of leprosy and disease as well as anyone who had been in contact with dead persons. These were all to be in isolation "out of the camp."

The idea here can be compared with our practice of quarantine. However, being put in quarantine, put outside the camp, was a most unpleasant and at times horrible experience even though there were the various provisions for cleansing that would restore the person to a place within the camp. Of primary importance, though, was the underlying truth that a holy God could not be approached in worship by a person who was unclean.

Now, let's shift the scene from the Sinai desert to the first century and the Good News in the Book of

Hebrews which refers to Jesus suffering "outside the gate" in order "that he might sanctify the people with his own blood" (Heb. 13:12). Here we have the picture of Jesus going outside the camp to make a cleansing sacrifice for everyone who is unclean. But the Hebrews writer then adds, "Let us go forth therefore unto him without the camp, bearing his reproach" (Heb. 13:13).

In Christ, there is redemption, even for those "outside the camp." No uncleanness can be so vile, no sin so horrendous, no estrangement so severe, that it is beyond the reach of Christ's redemptive love "outside the camp." That is the great Good News of the gospel!

From time to time as a pastor I become aware that someone who had always been faithful in church attendance has been missing. Recently, I called just such a person, and in response to my query, she said, "We've decided to get a divorce. It is a very messy situation, and I don't want to be a burden or an

A scene along the wilderness area through which the Hebrews likely traveled. Notice the lone tamarisk tree against the stark backdrop of the surrounding territory.

embarrassment to the church. I've decided that it is best for everyone if I just stay away."

In response I was able to assure her that this was exactly the time in her life that she needed the church—and the church needed her. With that she returned from "outside the camp" and began the process of healing.

The Making of Restitution (5:5–10)

The provision of these next six verses was given to provide a way of making right those sins and trespasses against the rights and property of another person. The underlying principle here is that to sin against another person is in fact sinning against God. How we live together in our human relationships is vital to our relationship with God.

To maintain purity and cleanness within the camp, such trespasses against another person had to be made right—restitution had to be made, not just for the amount defrauded or stolen, but a twenty percent surcharge was to be added. If the person who had been wronged could not be found, then the full amount must be paid to the nearest relative, and if that person could not be located, then payment was to be made to the priest.

The Law Governing Infidelity (5:11–31)

There is just no way we can identify with the situation described here. The scene focuses on a wife's being put to a test to determine her guilt or innocence of infidelity. It is a scene in which a woman under suspicion was subjected to a routine that was not only frightening and humiliating, but was one of ritual magic common also to many Near Eastern cultures of that time. Most certainly, this law would have been a powerful deterrent to marital infidelity. We do know, however, that this particular practice was modified in later laws.

But the important point being made here was that adultery, infidelity of any kind, was a horrible breach of the holiness of God. At all costs, purity in the Hebrew camp had to be safeguarded.

The Nazirite Vow (6:1–21)

The Numbers writer continues this log of miscellaneous laws with the provision for the "vow of a

Nazarite [Nazirite]." This is the first mention of Nazirites and the Nazirite vow in the Bible; however, Nazirites appear regularly in Israel's history.

The "nazir" was a man or woman who made a special vow to God that could either be in force for a short time or for the length of one's life. The prophet Amos, who was active around 750 B.C., ranked the Nazirites right alongside the prophets (Amos 2:11–12). One of the best-known early Nazirites in our Bible story was Samson, and centuries later John the Baptist was designated to be a Nazirite at the time of his birth.

Three Features of the Nazirite Vow

As we see from the details given in this part of our Scripture lesson, there were three features to the Nazirite vow: (1) a Nazirite must abstain from drinking wine or eating grapes (6:3–4); (2) his hair was not to be cut nor his beard shaved (6:5); and (3) he was not to touch a dead body (6:6).

As a person dedicated to God's service, the Nazirite would not experience the routine and comfortable style of life symbolized by wine and the fruit of the vine. He was to be a person of strength and dignity as symbolized by uncut hair and beard. And he must never touch a dead body because he was to be always ceremonially clean. However, the Nazirite was not to live in isolation but was to be an active participant in the life of Israel.

In verses 9 through 12 of this part of our Scripture lesson we find provision for purification of any Nazirite who accidently came in contact with a dead body. And in verses 13 through 21 we find the ceremonial ritual of sacrifices and offerings that were to be made upon the termination of a vow that was effective for a limited period of time.

For the twentieth-century Christian, much of this seems strange. It is, of course, a part of another time and of a drastically different world from ours today. Yet, there is much about the Nazirite symbolism that applies to us. As Christians, we are set apart—consecrated—to the Lord's service as members of His new society in our modern world. Jesus made it clear to

His followers that while they were *in* the world, they were not to be *of* the world. In a sense, we are not meant to settle down comfortably but are to ever be alert to our active role as sons and daughters of God. As Christians in a rather schizophrenic world, we are to conduct ourselves with a calm strength and quiet dignity that comes from faith in God, and we are to be clean and holy in our way of life and in relationship with our neighbors. There's much about the Nazirite vow and life-style when we understand it that has meaning for us.

This particular part of our Scripture lesson is concluded now with one of the most beautiful and poetic prayers in all of the Bible.

The prayer of benediction comes to us in three parts:

- The Lord bless thee, and keep thee;
- The Lord make his face shine upon thee, and be gracious unto thee;
- The Lord lift up his countenance upon thee, and give thee peace.

The Great Benediction (6:24–27)

This blessing invokes the love and power of God for the protection and preservation of His people, the grace of God for guidance and enlightenment, and the presence of God for our peace—the divine *shalom.* Unfortunately, our English word *peace* is most often used to express merely the absence of conflict or some general mood of serenity. But the Hebrew *shalom* is a far more comprehensive word, meaning health, well-being, wholeness, and completeness in all of life and our relationships.

To wish someone *shalom* is to want the very best of everything for that person. This *shalom* comes from God only when people are genuinely devoted to seeking and doing His will. *Shalom* was only possible for the ancient Hebrews when they were in tune with God's covenant love. It is always the promised gift of God to everyone who loves Him and keeps His commandments.

The Offerings of the "Princes of Israel" (Chapter 7)

In Chapter 5 of our Scripture lesson, God through Moses had emphasized the importance of purity in all of life's activities and relationships. Then, in Chapter 6 came the call for consecration and separation for God's service. Now, as we move into Chapter 7, our attention is directed to stewardship—the giving of offerings used in connection with our worship.

Only one section of our Old Testament is longer than this chapter—the 119th Psalm. On the surface these 89 verses are tedious and repetitious. But they exhibit for us once more God's care for detail in the preparation for worship. We see in these verses that no part of the Tabernacle worship was left to chance. It was too important for that.

In the early verses of the Book of Numbers we had the account of the numbering of the Hebrews. Also, in those verses were listed the names of the leaders or princes of each of the twelve tribes. Now, in this part of our Scripture lesson we have the detailed account of the offerings that were presented to the Lord by each of these tribal chieftains.

Each of these twelve leaders on consecutive days brought their offerings to God. There were six wagons and twelve oxen for use in transporting the Tabernacle and all of its equipment when the camp was on the move. Then came the offerings of the gold and silver vessels and all other equipment needed in the service of worship. All in all, it makes an impressive inventory list.

In reading these verses we get the picture of one long procession after another over a period of twelve days. In many ways the repetition is deadening until we see the bigger picture—a picture of an eager people who gave lavishly to their God everything that was needed for worship in His house. We read that they gave willingly—a model for us in the support of our churches and of missionary efforts across the world.

The climax to this progression of events is reached in verse 89. The Tabernacle was completed and properly furnished with all of the equipment and supplies—everything was in place. Then we read, "And when Moses was gone into the tabernacle of the congregation to speak with him [God], then he heard the voice of one speaking unto him from off the mercy seat that was upon the ark of the testimony, from between the two cherubims: and he spake unto him."

When Moses heard the voice of God from above the Ark, from the space between the outstretched wings of the cherubim, it signaled the completion of the place of worship. We also know that we are moving steadily closer to the beginning of the drama of the move north from the slopes of Mount Sinai toward the Promised Land. The presence of God was in the camp.

With everything in place, the Lord then gave Moses these instructions, "Speak unto Aaron, and say unto him, When thou lightest the lamps, the seven lamps shall give light over against the candlestick." The Golden Lampstand had been made according to the specifications given in Exodus 25:31–40 and described in Exodus 37:17–24. It was made all in one piece with a central shaft and six branches. At the end of each branch was a cup shaped like the flower of an almond tree that held the oil.

The Hebrew word for the Lampstand is *Menorah.* The *Menorah* is still one of the basic symbols of Judaism. The theme of light has always been central to the faith of biblical people. In the opening verses of his Gospel John said this about Jesus: "In him was life; and the life was the light of men. And the light shineth in the darkness; and the darkness comprehended it not [couldn't put it out]" (John 1:4–5). Later in the Gospel Jesus said, "I am the light of the world: he that followeth me shall not walk in darkness, but shall have the light of life" (John 8:12).

Then as we carry the light analogy a step further, we see that even as the Golden Lampstand symbolized the light of God in the place of worship in the center of the Hebrews' camp, so we are to let our light shine in our twentieth-century world so that

Setting Up the Lamps (8:1–4)

The Consecration of the Levites (8:5–26)

others come to know the living God as light and life (Matt. 5:14–16).

With the completion of the Tabernacle, the Levites who had been designated for special service in Numbers 3 and 4 are now cleansed and consecrated—set apart—for their work. The ritual of cleansing involved washing and shaving their bodies and washing their clothing. In addition a bullock was sacrificed as a sin offering and another bullock was sacrificed as a burnt offering.

But perhaps the ritual of the laying on of hands (8:10) has the most significance for us. Here is another ancient tradition that continues to be a part of our ritual today. In the Old Testament the laying on of hands always accompanied the giving of a blessing or the transfer of sin and guilt. Here it is obviously the giving of a blessing.

In the New Testament the laying on of hands is always associated with the giving of blessing. For example, we read that Jesus laid His hands upon the little children and blessed them (Matt. 19:13–15). Baptism was accompanied by the laying on of hands. Healing often involved the laying on of hands. And people were ordained or commissioned to ministry with the laying on of hands.

I am happy to say that there is a renewed emphasis in the church today on the laying on of hands on special occasions and for special needs. I believe this is a welcome recovery of an ancient tradition as long as we understand that there is no power within us that is transmitted. Only God can bless, and we can recognize and affirm that truth by the laying on of hands with prayer.

The Second Passover (9:1–14)

The Hebrews had spent a year at the foot of Mount Sinai, the mountain of God. Now the instructions are given for the celebration of their second Passover—their first as a free people. You will recall that the first Passover was observed while they were still in bondage in Egypt. Since then, it has been celebrated annually by faithful Jews.

The modern Jewish Passover blends various traditions that have accumulated over the centuries. Unleavened bread brings to mind that there was no time for the leavening process because of the haste in which the Hebrews left Egypt. Part of the shankbone of a lamb is roasted, a symbol of the lambs offered in the Tabernacle and later in the Temple. It is also a reminder of the lamb that was slaughtered and provided blood to mark the side and upper doorposts so the angel of death would pass over their homes without striking the firstborn. Then there is the roasted egg to symbolize the new life that emerges out of disaster through God's grace. Bitter herbs symbolize their former slavery in Egypt, and sweet fruits recall God's kindness and faithful love. In the celebration of the Passover the Jewish people are reminded that their faith is rooted in God's action in history.

In similar fashion, the sacrament of the Lord's Supper serves as a reminder that Christ became our Passover Lamb (1 Cor. 5:7). Jesus is the Lamb of God sacrificed for our sins. In this we see God's action in our history. When Jesus broke the bread and took the cup and offered them to His disciples, He said, "This is my body which is given for you. . . . This cup is the new testament in my blood, which is shed for you" (Luke 22:19–20).

God's Unfailing Guidance (9:15–23)

We have been moving steadily in our study so far toward that climactic time when word would be given for the camp of Israel to move away from Mount Sinai. With the celebration of the second Passover the stage was pretty well set. So now, we come to what must have been a most dramatic moment. The Numbers writer describes it in these words: "And on the day that the tabernacle was reared up the cloud covered the tabernacle, namely, the tent of the testimony: and at even there was upon the tabernacle as it were the appearance of fire, until the morning. So it was alway: the cloud covered it by day, and the appearance of fire by night" (9:15–16).

Here we have the vivid description of one of the most dramatic symbols of God's grace to His people. While numerous explanations of this phenomenon have been attempted, it seems obvious to me that it is best to regard this as one of the mysteries of God's presence with and guidance of His people. We first read of the cloud when the Hebrews left Egypt (Exod. 13:21–22), and it guided the people to Mount Sinai. And there it hovered over the mountain as the Covenant was given to Moses (Exod. 19:16; 24:15–18).

This cloud and its luminous form at night was to guide them. The instructions were clear. When the cloud moved forward, the people moved; when the cloud stopped, they stopped. There were times when the cloud stopped just long enough for a one night camp, but other times it lingered in one spot for days and even weeks.

While we're not blessed with a visible cloud to guide us, this ancient symbol is a reminder of our need for God's guidance. I'll admit there have been times when I would have taken great comfort in physically seeing God's cloud pointing the way for me. But then I am reminded that I have One who promised, "Lo, I am with you alway, even unto the end of the world" (Matt. 28:20). Through prayer, study, and the counsel of my fellow Christians I have my "cloud of guidance."

The Silver Trumpets (10:1–10)

In this final set of instructions to make "two trumpets of silver," the Lord provides the means for sending direction signals to the entire encampment. These trumpets were simple instruments from one to three feet in length, but they served as guidance for the peoples' actions.

A code was provided. A sharp blast of both trumpets was the signal for the entire camp to assemble together (10:3). A blast from just one trumpet was the call for the tribal leaders to meet (10:4). Different combinations of notes signaled movement forward, an alarm in event of danger, a call to battle, the announcement of special days, festivals and times of sacrifice (10:5–10).

Again, we can't help but be amazed and also reassured at the effort God took to make certain His people were cared for. No detail of their movements was to be left to chance; they would be guided with each forward step. And when the last of the instructions for travel had been given, God reminded His people, "I am the Lord your God" (10:10b).

Through the movement of the cloud and the sounds of the silver trumpets, God's will and purpose were conveyed to every Hebrew in the camp. None was left to wonder. In all of this, we are reminded that God's Spirit doesn't give guidance to just a few. It is there for all of us as we seek to know His will and watch and listen for our guidance. And we have the same assurance that He gave to our spiritual ancestors at the foot of Mount Sinai: "I am the Lord your God."

Loving Lord, Thank You for guiding me, step by step. Even when I can't sense Your leading, I know You're arranging things according to Your plan. Thank You for not leaving me alone. Amen.

WHAT THIS SCRIPTURE MEANS TO ME
Numbers 1—10:10

Every summer at camp, on the first morning of Round Up, all the campers and counselors got out of bed at dawn, before reveille. I remember the cool air and the steam rising from the surface of the Guadalupe River. In total silence, as our hearts pounded with anticipation of the final camp games, we put on our tribe colors and met at our special appointed places.

We had prepared for Round Up for five weeks. We had learned how to play the games, and we had also learned well the rules of good sportsmanship. No matter who won or lost, each camper who had followed the camp rules would receive an award.

When the bugle of reveille blew, we were ready and bursting with excitement. At the first note, both tribes broke into a march, chanting and singing around the campsite. We were led by the tribe captain wearing her headdress, the symbol of authority.

As I read our Scripture lesson, I can identify with the Israelites as they prepared to set out on their journey to the Promised Land. In the lesson, we see them making sure everybody is accounted for and in their special place. Then they are given the camp laws and final instructions. Next Aaron gives them a blessing. And then we can almost feel their tingling excitement as they wait for the notes of the silver trumpet. On to the Promised Land at last!

Today, as we go through life on our own spiritual journeys, some moments are as thrilling as that day for the Israelites. The "highs" in my own life include my confirmation when I was twelve, my reconversion as an adult, and several retreat weekends when I felt as if I were starting out all over again to the Promised Land.

However, a lot of my journey is and has been much more ordinary. I get bogged down in the routine of life, and like the Israelites, I start to grumble about day-to-day things. I lose the quickened pulse of God's love, and the sense of the adventure of life in Him.

Yet, as we see in the lesson, God provides for our burnout and our discouragement. His love guided the Israelites in the form of a pillar of cloud by day and a pillar of fire by night. The fire and the cloud were visible reminders that God was present with them day and night.

Though today we do not have a pillar of fire or cloud to lead us, God has provided us with a Guide and a Comfortor. The Holy Spirit is present with us day and night, a manifestation of God's love for us.

Several years ago, I found myself in a desert of discouragement. My husband's and my efforts to have a child weren't working out and my job had become routine. My spiritual life had lost its zip. I felt listless and depressed. Searching for God's will for my life had become like groping in the dark without a flashlight.

Then, one evening after praying especially hard for guidance, I was reading in the Psalms. Suddenly an idea occurred to me—I could go to seminary to study and be a teacher! It was almost as clear as a pillar of fire in my bedroom. I knew the Holy Spirit was answering my prayer.

Seminary proved to be a stimulating adventure in itself. But the main thing I learned was the same lesson God taught the Israelites as they prepared to embark on their journey to the Promised Land. God is present with us even when the thrill wears off. In exciting times and in discouraging times, He leads us, guides us, and loves us.

LESSON 4
Numbers 10:11–20:13

On the Road

Dear Lord, When my life seems like a frustrating journey in the wilderness, help me to remember Your faithfulness to Your people long ago and to trust Your love which never fails. AMEN.

The great moment has arrived! For almost a year, the Hebrew people have been in one place in the "wilderness of Sinai," receiving instructions as to worship and living in preparation for their journey to the Promised Land, the land of Canaan. In Exodus 19:1 we learned that they arrived at Sinai in the third month of their first year of freedom from Egypt. Now, on the twentieth day of the second month of the second year of their freedom, they break camp and move out.

In our previous study, we learned that the first ten chapters of Numbers dealt with the final twenty days of that period of waiting. I can easily imagine their feelings of impatience and their eagerness to move on. Still vivid in their memories were the exciting events of their liberation—the drama of the Passover, the hasty departure from Egypt, the pursuit by the Egyptian army, the terror of being trapped, the miraculous parting of the waters, the watery death of the Egyptians, the remarkable provision of food and water, the celebration of liberation from bondage. But then they had a year of waiting for God's marching orders.

This pattern is more characteristic of life with God than we like to accept. A nineteenth-century preacher, Phillips Brooks, often said, "My problem is that I am always in a hurry, but God never seems to be!" Again and again, we are urged to "wait upon the Lord." Waiting for God is a normal requirement for the people of God. Even after the exciting events surrounding the death and resurrection of Jesus, He instructed His disciples to *wait* in Jerusalem until the coming of the Holy Spirit.

In this section of Numbers, we will discover that these ten chapters cover a period of some thirty-eight years of another kind of waiting. In fact, the abiding lesson of the Book of Numbers has to be the importance of learning to wait on God and trust in Him. And for us folks who are geared to life in the fast lane with fast food outlets, microwave ovens, and instant color photographs, this is no small assignment. But it wasn't any easier for the people of Israel than it is for us.

The thread that ties the stories of these ten chapters together is the theme of "murmuring." People who vacillate in their faith invariably end up mumbling and grumbling. Such an honest and debasing self-portrayal attests to the credibility of these stories. And, at the same time we catch a vivid picture of God at work in and through everything that happens. The central subject of the story is neither Moses nor the Hebrew people; it is God. The ultimate triumph over the wilderness and the conquest of Canaan will be won, not by military might, brilliant strategy, or exceptional bravery, but by the love and action of God.

The Journey Begins (10:11–36)
The Order of March

As the cloud lifts from above the Tabernacle (10:11), the Hebrew people moved out according to the instructions already given in Chapter 2, except the Levites were divided into two sections. The Gershonites and the Merarites dismantled the outer parts of the Tabernacle and its courtyard and followed immediately after the three lead tribes—Judah, Issachar, and Zebulun. Next came the tribes of Reuben, Simeon, and Gad. And behind them came the rest of the Levites—the Kohathites—who were carrying "the sanctuary," a probable reference to the furnishings of the Tabernacle. Then, behind them followed the remaining tribes, with Dan as the rear guard.

The order of march as spelled out in these verses (10:14–27) served a utilitarian purpose. With the Gershonites and the Merarites at the head of the column, it meant that when they stopped, the Tabernacle structure could be set in place before the Kohathites arrived with the holy things—the furnishings. Again, we are impressed by God's attention to order and detail.

The First Major Stop

With no other detail, we are told that "the children of Israel took their journeys out of the wilderness of Sinai; and the cloud rested *in the wilderness of Paran*" (10:12, italics mine). Their first major stop, the wilderness of Paran, cannot be located precisely, but the name has survived among some of the Bedouin tribes to this very day. But wherever it was, it was still wilderness!

God didn't move them from the wilderness of Sinai into a land "flowing with milk and honey" in one jump. Many preachers and teachers over the centuries have drawn parallels between the Christian life and the experience of the children of Israel in the wilderness. And there *are* parallels—we, too, in our journey of faith seem to move from one wilderness to another—from our personal Sinai to Paran.

For the Hebrews, the thrill of breaking camp after a year of waiting didn't mean that their next major stop would be the Promised Land. There's always the danger that we view high moments in our spiritual experience as the end of a dry spell in our journey—only to find that we have entered another wilderness. But as children of God, our confidence must be in God, whether we are in the wilderness or the Promised Land.

Next we come to a rather fascinating human interest story, the discussion between Moses and Hobab (10:29–32). Our King James text refers to Hobab as "the son of Raguel." The reference is undoubtedly to Reuel or Jethro, Moses' father-in-law (Exod. 2:18–22; 3:1). This would make Hobab Moses' brother-in-law even though there is some confusion caused by certain later references to him.

Here we see Moses asking Hobab to be their human guide through the wilderness journey. In this request we sense both the wisdom and humility of Moses in asking for the help of an outsider—a Midianite or Kenite. Moses was keenly aware of his need for someone who knew and understood the desert for the long journey ahead. Even though Moses heard directly from God, it seems that he used good common sense in asking the desert-wise Hobab for help. I just have to believe there are times when God sends human counsel to us in our moments of need.

According to the story, Moses' first approach to Hobab was aimed at his self-interest, "We are journeying unto the place of which the Lord said, I will give it you: come thou with us, *and we will do thee good:* for the Lord hath spoken good concerning Israel" (10:29, italics mine). Hobab refused. But then Moses appealed to his own need for help—"thou mayest be to us instead of eyes" (10:31b). Evidently this appeal was successful for it would appear from the wording of Judges 1:16 that Hobab stayed with them.

I find this exchange between Moses and his brother-in-law most intriguing. It causes me to wonder just how often I go at somebody with the idea that I am doing them a favor. I've seen Christians, as I'm sure you have, who adopt somewhat of a patronizing attitude toward unbelievers. Such a spirit tends to repel people and renders our witness invalid.

There has been considerable speculation as to the precise meaning of verses 33 through 36 in this part of our Scripture lesson. For our purposes I believe it

A Human Guide Acquired

The Ark and God's Guidance

93

Sights such as the one pictured here were familiar to the people of Israel as they traveled from Mount Sinai to the wilderness of Paran.

is sufficient to say that the central idea here is that God's presence with the Hebrews was assured both by the "cloud of the Lord" and by the Ark of the Covenant. God was there to guide them; He was in their midst at all times. This they could count on. The close identity of the Ark with God's presence will continue to be central to the story.

While we do not have the cloud or the Ark to visually assure us of God's presence and guidance, our faith is firmly fixed in the reassuring promises of Jesus. We can count on His presence because He Himself said, "I will pray the Father, and he shall give you another Comforter. . . . I will not leave you comfortless; I will come to you" (John 14:16–18).

We catch our first real glimpse now in this part of the story of the mood of the Hebrews when the going gets tough. We have a story of stress and strain, of mumbling and grumbling. In a way it is an understandable story because the journey was tough and demanding. The terrain was rocky and mountainous—anything but friendly. Evidently they had expected an easier road.

So they complained; they mumbled and grumbled. Underlying all of their complaining was an assumption all too common today—God always gives comfort, happiness, and success. The idea that God might lead His people to hardship and sacrifice was utterly incomprehensible to them. They expected God to get them out of scrapes, not lead them into them. Today we tend to buy into the "Christian success syndrome," and find it dreadfully hard to understand that God works in *everything* for our good—even the hardships and apparent reverses.

Stress and Strain on the Journey (Chapter 11)

The Hebrews hadn't been on the road long before their complaining and griping "displeased the Lord" (11:1). It must have been pretty bad because God had been extremely patient with them. But the Numbers writer tells us that the Lord was so displeased with their attitude that "his anger was kindled; and the fire of the Lord burnt among them, and consumed them that were in the uttermost parts of the camp."

When this happened, we're told that "the people cried unto Moses; and when Moses prayed unto the Lord, the fire was quenched" (11:2). In other words, when Moses interceded in their behalf, relief arrived. This is pretty much the scenario in all of the stories that follow.

Then in the third verse we are told that Moses named this particular campsite Taberah, a Hebrew word that means "burning" (11:3).

Fire is often seen as a symbol of God's presence and power. The fire of the burning bush was a sign

"He Called the Name of the Place Taberah"

of God's speaking. At Sinai fire was a symbol of God's glorious presence. On other occasions it is a symbol of His purging power or of His anger. The writer of the Book of Deuteronomy describes God in these words, "For the Lord thy God is a consuming fire, even a jealous God" (4:24).

But the fire of God's anger must always be seen as anger at sin and not at the sinner. Dr. Sam Shoemaker, gifted Episcopal rector in New York and Pittsburgh a generation ago, was fond of saying that God hates the sin but loves the sinner. God's anger against sin is seen as disciplining, cleansing, educating, renewing. It is always designed to restore the relationship that has been broken by sin.

Complaints About Food

Sometimes it takes only a few malcontents to sour the mood of a whole community. This next scene (11:4–9) reminds me of my years in the Marine Corps during the second World War. There the most common complaints were about the food. In reality, most of us were not all that hard to please, but as soon as a few began to complain about the "mess," almost everyone else joined in.

That's what happened to Moses now. A few people, referred to in the King James text as "a mixt multitude" and in some modern translations as "the rabble," stirred up the crowd over the food. Their daily needs were being adequately met by the manna, thought to be a gumlike substance from a desert shrub that builds up during the night and drops to the ground. The Bedouin still use it today and spread it on bread like jam. From the description in Exodus 16:15 we know that when the people first saw this substance on the ground, they asked, "What is it?"—man hu in Hebrew, and from this it came to be called manna.

As we look closely at the details of this story, we discover that the Hebrews weren't grumbling and complaining because they were hungry. They were just tired of their plain diet—the same old thing day after day. The teller of our story paints a pretty clear picture of their attitude and wants, "Who shall give us flesh to eat? We remember the fish, which we did eat in Egypt freely; the cucumbers, and the melons, and the leeks, and the onions, and the garlick" (11:4b–5).

Their recollection of these "exotic" foods in Egypt now blocked out the misery of their bondage, so that those years became "the good old days." Our memories are selective, aren't they? When we get to complaining about the way things are, we tend to rewrite the way things were and remember only pleasant things. When viewed realistically, the "good old days" weren't quite as good as we make them out to be. And when we start living in the re-created past, we're likely to miss what is good in the present.

As we read verses 10 through 15, we see a very human Moses. He had listened to the people's gripes and complaints, and he had seen the anger of the Lord. He had had it! And so he began to feel really sorry for himself. Faced with God's anger and the people's fickleness, he felt trapped and utterly alone. His task was impossible. It is even possible in this moment of acute depression that he wished he had never taken the voice from the burning bush seriously.

Moses was so engrossed in his misery that he didn't even think to ask for help. The Numbers writer catches his strong feeling with these words, "I am not able to bear [stand] all this people alone, because it is too heavy for me. And if thou deal thus with me, *kill me,* I pray thee, out of hand, if I have found favour in thy sight; and let me not see my wretchedness" (11:14–15, italics mine). Imagine! Moses was so despondent that he asked the Lord to kill him.

Can you identify with Moses at this point? I can. Most of us, I'm sure, have confronted seemingly insurmountable difficulties in our marriages, in family relationships, in work and business responsibilities, and even in our church relationships. We feel we've done the best we could and failed, and so we blame God and feel sorry for ourselves.

The story of Moses gives me great encouragement. It is good to know that God can handle our criticism

Moses Complains

and complaints. There was a time when I was afraid to argue with God, much less criticize Him. Not long after my father died at sixty-four, I experienced a growing anger with God. Dad had never had much materially. He worked hard as a bus driver, saving what little he could for his retirement years, with dreams of travel and leisure. And then came the cancer, and death, and unrealized dreams and hopes. It seemed so unfair. But how do you question God?

One afternoon, after conducting a burial service at the cemetery where Dad was buried, I walked alone to his grave site. As I stood there, I felt a surge of anger, and I spoke some frank and disparaging words to God. In a rage, I kicked the gravestone. And then, a quiet calm came within. I felt as though God were saying to me, "It's all right, my son. I feel your pain. I know your hurt. Take my hand and stay close. I want to be your strength and comfort."

As a result of this experience, I'll never doubt again that we have a God with whom we can be frankly honest. He can take our anger and not condemn us. He can handle our criticism and give us strength. He can field our self-pity and turn it into constructive action. There is nothing we can do which will exhaust God's unfailing love.

God Responds to Moses

Once again we see the wonderful patience of the Lord. He understood Moses' feelings, as He now responds both to Moses' desperation over trying to lead the people alone and to the Hebrews' complaint about their diet (11:16–23).

First God told Moses to select seventy men who were established and trusted leaders and assemble them at the front of the Tabernacle. And when they were all assembled, God said He would speak to them and commission their leadership (11:16–17).

Second, God told Moses that he would send meat and the people were to eat it every day for a whole month until they became sick of it (11:18–20). Moses is amazed at this word from the Lord and questions where all of this "flesh" will come from, only to hear God say, "Is the Lord's hand waxed short [is there a limit to the Lord's power]? thou shalt see now whether my word shall come to pass unto thee or not" (11:23).

As soon as the Lord finished telling Moses what to do and promising what He would do about the food problem, Moses passed on the word of the Lord to the people. He also selected the seventy men who were to share his burden of leadership (11:24–30). As they stood around the Tabernacle, God consecrated the leaders, and we're told that when the Spirit of the Lord came upon them "they prophesied"—presumably a kind of Spirit-filled ecstasy which later came to be associated with the early prophets (1 Sam. 10:10–12; 19:20–24). As near as we can tell, this sign was only given to them once and wasn't repeated—it was temporary.

There's an interesting "aside" to this story as the writer briefly mentions two of the seventy who for some reason did not meet with the others at the front of the Tabernacle. The two were named Eldad and Medad, and even though they weren't with the others, they too were given the prophesying gift. When word of this reached Moses, Joshua, who was with him, said, "My lord Moses, forbid them" (11:28). Joshua wanted Moses to tell them to stop because they were not with the rest of the elders and with Moses at the Tabernacle.

Moses' reply to Joshua is one of the classic statements in our Bible, "Enviest thou for my sake? would God that all the Lord's people were prophets, and that the Lord would put his spirit upon them!" (11:29). There was nothing narrow or parochial about Moses at this point, but not until the great Day of Pentecost centuries later would Moses' dream become a reality (Acts 2). How cautious we need to be to not exclude or condemn those faithful believers whose understanding of the faith is different from ours, or who do not belong to our group.

At the time of the Protestant Reformation in the seventeenth century, great emphasis was laid on the "priesthood of all believers." I wonder if the time has not arrived now in these closing days of the twentieth century for an emphasis on the "prophethood

Moses Acts on God's Instructions

of all believers"? After all, a prophet is one who speaks for God. I believe God calls all of us to be prophets—laypersons and clergy alike. We are all witnesses, both by our words and our actions.

The Lord Sends the Quail

Now, in the concluding verses of Chapter 11 the Lord makes good His promise to send meat (11:31–35). The story writer describes what happened. "And there went forth a wind from the Lord, and brought quails from the sea, and let them fall by the camp." This could well have been a part of an annual occurrence in that part of the world. During March and April great flocks of quail migrate eastward across the Sinai peninsula and then return again in September on their way back south. They fly close to the ground for short distances at a time and are netted in great quantities.

But however this action of God occurred, He acted, and they had quail in superabundance. In fact, we read that they gorged themselves. The story is one of excessive gluttony that was followed by a severe plague of illness that took many lives. In fact, we read that Moses called the name of the place where this happened Kibroth-hattaavah—"graves of craving"—"because there they buried the people that lusted."

There's something about this scene that speaks to our condition today. Ours is a society of affluence. So often we strive for those things we feel are important, only to succeed to the point of acquiring in excess. We strive for material gain and for position and status, and in that insatiable striving we all too often become masters of our own destruction. We are consumed by a lust for second homes, for boats and recreational vehicles. All too often our lust for things is so great that it consumes all of our resources and energy while at the same time people in many parts of the world are hungry and starving and are victims of disease because there aren't medical supplies and doctors.

The picture at Kibroth-hattaavah in the Sinai peninsula is a tragic portrayal of the results of dissatisfaction and complaining. It exposes the cancer of misplaced values and of the insatiable lust for "more." As for the Hebrews, I'm sure they were glad to move on "from Kibroth-hattaavah unto Hazeroth," where they set up camp again (11:35).

The action is interrupted now as we are taken behind the scenes into the inner circle of Moses and his brother and sister, Aaron and Miriam.

A Family Quarrel (Chapter 12)

Jealousy Disrupts Their Relationship

While Aaron is involved, it is obvious that Miriam is the ringleader because of strong feelings of jealousy. And somehow, jealousy is at its worst among religious leaders. We know from other references that Miriam was a prophetess (Exod. 15:20) and Aaron had been designated as the spokesperson for the children of Israel (Exod. 4:14–16).

For very human reasons Miriam and Aaron had come to resent the fact that God spoke in unique ways to Moses, overshadowing their own roles and positions. The opening words of the story give us the excuse for the attack of Miriam and Aaron on Moses. It was "because of the Ethiopian woman whom he had married." But then the real reason follows almost immediately. They were jealous of Moses' special relationship with the Lord (12:2). Because of this, they wanted to cut Moses down to size—to put him down. They suffered from the mistaken idea that the best way to get the recognition they thought they deserved was to undercut Moses. But that never works.

The Cancer of Jealousy in Religious Leadership

I'll never forget a lesson I learned many years ago when I was just a young minister. It happened in a conversation with a group of people. The ministry of a well-known television evangelist was being discussed, and I went on at great lengths expressing my negative views of him and his ministry. Unquestionably, my vehemence at the time was salted with sharp doses of jealousy.

A very wise layperson who had also been a part of the conversation took me aside later and said privately, "Son, I hope someday you'll learn that God called you to be in sales and not in management."

The wisdom wrapped up in those few words has stayed with me through the years.

Qualities of Greatness

Having given the reasons for the attack on Moses by his brother and sister, the writer now includes a brief parenthesis that tells us a lot about what has happened to Moses under the Lord's leading, "(Now the man Moses was very meek, above all the men which were upon the face of the earth)" (12:3). Then in the rest of Chapter 12 we see how God handled the insurrection.

The statement in parentheses, though, is given greater emphasis when we read in verse 13 how Moses responded to God's judgment of Miriam, "Heal her now, O God, I beseech thee." Too often meekness is thought of as timidity and a lack of assertiveness. Not so! Meekness is that quiet strength that never needs to bluff or bully. In the Beatitudes, Jesus indicated that the meek would inherit the earth. Jesus Himself was the model of meekness, ever exuding an aura of inner strength and power, as on the day when He walked through a hostile crowd intent on killing Him, without incident (Luke 4:28–30). Meekness is not weakness.

The Tragic Blunder (Chapters 13–14)

Our next scene has the children of Israel encamped at Kadesh in the wilderness of Paran (13:26). They were on the threshold of that to which God had called them—the occupation of the Promised Land. Taking and occupying the land from the south was the logical move. But, as we shall now see, they failed to trust God in the crucial moment and turned to their own human calculations and assumptions, ending in a tragic defeat by the Amalekites and Canaanites who lived in the southern hill country (14:44–45). As a result of their disobedience, it was God's decree that the entire generation of people would spend their lives in the wilderness (forty years). The conquering and occupation of Canaan would await a new generation.

This part of our Scripture lesson weaves together different emphases of the events with special focus upon the inner meaning that they had for Moses and the people.

In sending the tribal leaders as spies to survey Canaan, the Lord wanted to assure the people that the land was indeed desirable (13:1–24). We learn in the description that they had gone as far north as Hebron. However, it is possible they may have traveled much further north. The place called Rehob (13:21) has never been located.

The Sending of Spies

The forty-day exploratory trip of the twelve spies enabled them to report that the land was rich and fertile—a land that flowed "with milk and honey" (13:25–33). There was complete agreement about the richness of the land, but at the same time there was a vigorous difference among the twelve in their opinion about the strength of the inhabitants. Joshua and Caleb brought in a positive report. Caleb's words have been preserved for us, "Let us go up at once, and possess it; for we are well able to overcome it" (13:30).

Report of the Spies

However, the other ten spies brought in a negative and gloomy report. "We be not able to go up against the people; for they are stronger than we" (13:31). Then, the majority and negative report concluded with these words, "And there [in Canaan] we saw the giants, the sons of Anak, which come of the giants: *and we were in our own sight as grasshoppers,* and so we were in their sight" (13:33, italics mine).

There was the clincher. Those ten men, instead of seeing themselves as people of God, saw themselves as grasshoppers in a world of giants, and they caved in. Two of the spies saw the big picture; they saw God at work in the world. They remembered the miracle of the Exodus and God's step-by-step care of them every day while they were in the Sinai wilderness. They were convinced that their God would give them victory. But the other ten had forgotten God's faithfulness in the past and saw themselves as losers.

At our point in Christian history it is easy to be critical of those ten spies. Yet, how often we cave in before giant difficulties; we look in the mirror and see grasshoppers, and fail to occupy our land of promise. The great faith-antidote to the grasshopper syndrome was expressed so beautifully for us by the Apostle Paul when he wrote these words to his friends in Philippi, "I can do all things through Christ which strengtheneth me" (Phil. 4:13).

"Let Us Return into Egypt"

The response of the Hebrews favored the majority report. Their immediate reaction was "let us return into Egypt" (14:4). And they even went so far as to threaten Caleb and Joshua with death (14:10). Moses, Aaron, Joshua and Caleb all pleaded with the people not to rebel against the Lord, but without success.

Once again because of their disobedience the Lord threatened them with extinction, and once again Moses intervened and saved them (14:11–20). But judgment was pronounced—none of that generation but Caleb and Joshua would live to see the Promised Land. The children of Israel would remain in the wilderness until that entire generation died (14:21–35).

When the full meaning of this judgment seeped into their rebellious minds, the Hebrews were horror-stricken. They immediately reversed themselves and prepared to move forward. But it was too late. God had spoken. They must remain in the wilderness until the present generation was dead. But once again, they defied the Lord, and by trying to invade the land met crushing defeat from the Amalekite army. And so ends one of the saddest and most tragic chapters in the history of the children of Israel.

Miscellaneous Ritual Observances (Chapter 15)

Chapter 14 of our Scripture lesson ended with dismal defeat. Rebellion and disobedience kept the Hebrews out of their Promised Land, and now they were consigned to spend years in the wilderness—a bleak picture. But as we move into this part of the lesson, we see a bright ray of hope. While the present generation was written off and destined to die in the wilderness, there was still hope for the people as a nation. We have this assurance in the opening words of Chapter 15, "And the Lord spake unto Moses, saying, Speak unto the children of Israel, and say unto them, *When ye be come into the land of your habitations, which I give unto you . . .*" (15:1–2, italics mine). In other words, the promise remained good. At some future time they would possess the land.

Then follow five sections having to do with certain rituals of worship that are to be observed when they occupy Canaan. The primary concern of the first section is with the proper amounts of flour, wine, and oil to be used in connection with the burnt offerings and the peace offerings (15:3–16). These regulations are supplemental to those given in Leviticus 2 and 6.

The second section offers instructions pertaining to the offering of the coarse meal from the threshing floor at harvest time (15:17–21). The section on sins committed unknowingly (15:22–28) should be compared with Leviticus 4:1–5:13. These are portrayed in contrast to those sins done "with a high hand [presumptuously]" for which there was no sacrifice. The intentional breaking of the Sabbath was an example of "high-handed" sin, punishable by death (15:29–36).

The final section of Chapter 15, verses 37 through 41 provides a means for remembering the commands of the Lord. Reference is made in these verses to fringes or tassels that were to be secured by a blue cord. These served as visual-aid reminders that they are to follow the laws prescribed here.

I have known people who carry some form of reminder of their commitment to God. For example, John Wooden, former basketball coach of UCLA, always carries a little wooden cross in his pocket. Few people are even aware that he has it. But he says that every time he puts his hand in his pocket and feels that cross, he is reminded of who he is and whom he serves. To Coach Wooden his little cross is the equivalent of the tassles on the hem of the Hebrews' garments. The primary purpose of any and all such reminders point to the ultimate reality of our lives as expressed in verse 41, "I am the Lord your God, which brought you out of the land of Egypt, to be your God: I am the Lord your God."

Two excellent views of the terrain in ancient Edom—that part
of the wilderness to the west of the southern tip of the Dead Sea.
The people of Edom were descendents of Esau.

The Great Rebellion (Chapters 16–17)

As if the grumbling and complaining of the people wasn't tough enough on Moses, he is next faced with a full-scale rebellion and attempted revolution. As you read these two chapters of this part of our Scripture lesson, you will become aware that there are at least two plots woven together. Korah and some Levites attempted an overthrow of the exclusive right of Aaron and his sons to the priesthood. And Dathan and Abiram, descendants of Jacob's firstborn son, rebelled against the authority of Moses. These were revolutionary situations, the first involving 250 male members of the community council, and in the second situation Moses is accused of setting himself up as a prince (16:13).

The Rebellion of Korah

In the rebellion led by Korah, it was claimed that all Israelites had equal standing before God, and no one, not even Aaron, had a right to assume a special relationship with God (16:1–11, 16–19, 35). Korah and his 250 rebels were challenged by Moses each to take a censer and stand at the entrance of the Tabernacle. When they did, fire came down from God and consumed them.

Their censers were taken up by Eleazar, son of Aaron, and hammered into a bronze covering for the altar, a constant reminder of the failure of this revolutionary effort (16:36–40).

As the people complained against Moses, a plague quickly spread among them, but Aaron ran quickly with his burning censer into the middle of the crowd, standing "between the dead and the living," making an atonement, and stopping the plague (16:41–50).

The Rebellion of Dathan and Abiram

The rebellion led by two Reubenites, Dathan and Abiram, was an effort to overthrow Moses (16:12–15, 23–34). Not only did they accuse Moses of usurping the authority of a prince, but they charged him with failure to fulfill his promises and duties to bring them into the Promised Land. They based their case on the inability of Moses to deliver the good things of Canaan. They even accused Moses of having brought them *out* of a land "flowing with milk and honey," implying that their bondage in Egypt was preferable to their present state in the wilderness. Interestingly, their appeal was democratic, insisting that the authority of Moses derived from the people, not from God.

Moses protested to the Lord, defending his integrity and faithfulness. The rebels refused to respond to the challenge of Moses for an open confrontation, and God's judgment came with frightening results: the earth opened and swallowed both families!

*Moses' Authority Is
Confirmed*

In both situations, Moses put his trust completely in the Lord. And when God disciplined the people for their rebelliousness, Moses was still interceding for them. The leadership and authority of Moses is confirmed, and the continuing priesthood of Aaron is reaffirmed in the story of the budding of Aaron's rod as it is told in Chapter 17.

The ultimate question underlying Chapters 16 and 17 is that of authority. For those of us privileged to live within a political system in which the authority of government is "of the people, by the people, and for the people," a word of caution is in order at this point. While our democratic system is certainly preferable in our social and political society, we need to understand that God's Kingdom is based on theocracy—He is sovereign Lord and King, not some representative elected by the people. The Laws given by God for His spiritual Kingdom are absolutes and are not determined by the will of the majority of the people. In other words, the Kingdom of God is not based on democratic principles. But God's Kingdom and national governments are two completely different things.

**Duties and Privileges of
Priests and Levites
(Chapter 18)**

The obvious conclusion growing out of the rebellion of Korah, Dathan and Abiram, along with the fascinating story of the blossoms that bloomed on Aaron's rod as colorfully described in Chapter 17, is a powerful confirmation of Aaron's priesthood and the selection of the tribe of Levi to serve in the Tabernacle.

Chapter 17 ends with the mass acknowledgment of the people that anyone not appointed by God to serve in the Tabernacle faced death. Their question, "Shall we be consumed with dying?" called for an answer, and that answer comes now in this part of our Scripture lesson. It is clear that those appointed by God—Aaron and the Levites—are to minister in behalf of the people.

The various duties outlined here in Chapter 18 related to the sacrifices and worship and the care of the Tabernacle and its furnishings have already been established in Leviticus 1–7 and in Numbers 1–4 and 8. But it is also made clear here that all of those who spend their time in performance of the sacred duties associated with worship are to be maintained by a share or tithe of the offerings brought to God.

Paul reaffirmed this ancient principle for the Christian community when he told his Christian friends in Corinth, "Even so hath the Lord ordained that they which preach the gospel should live of the gospel [their living should be earned by the Christians to whom they minister]" (1 Cor. 9:14).

The Purifying Water (Chapter 19)

This particular part of our Scripture lesson relates to the various regulations studied in Lesson 1 in which we examined the ritual-laws found in Leviticus 11–15. There is some uncertainty from our perspective as to why this subject is picked up again here since it does not seem to be related either to what has gone on just before or what follows. Perhaps it comes here because there had been so much death in the camp that the people needed to be purified from their contact with dead bodies. But the provisions outlined so carefully now are for the purification water that was to be used in the cleansing process of a person who had become ceremonially unclean because of contact with a dead body.

The provisions for this particular law called for a red heifer to be killed "outside the camp" for a sin offering. Then the priest, instead of sprinkling the blood on the Altar, sprinkled it toward "the tabernacle of the congregation seven times" (19:4). Next, the heifer was burned and the ashes were carefully collected and stored in a clean place outside the camp.

When a ceremonially unclean person was to undergo the rites of purification, some of the ashes were mixed with clean water. This water was then sprinkled on the unclean person on the third and seventh day after he or she was defiled. By following the provisions laid out here, the person then became ceremonially clean again.

**A New Testament
Contrast**

The writer of the New Testament Book of Hebrews draws a sharp contrast between these kinds of rites and sacrifices and the sacrifice of Jesus Christ when he writes, "For if the blood of bulls and of goats, and the ashes of an heifer sprinkling the unclean, sanctifieth to the purifying of the flesh: How much more shall the blood of Christ, who through the eternal Spirit offered himself without spot to God, purge your conscience from dead works to serve the living God?" (Heb. 9:13–14).

**The Sin of Moses
(20:1–13)**
Out of Water

In this closing scene of our lesson we find the children of Israel camped at Kadesh in the "desert of Zin." It was there Miriam, Moses' sister, died. Then the Numbers writer moves ahead quickly and gives us a sad and tragic episode. This was another time when the Hebrews murmured and grumbled. The water supply was exhausted and they turned on Moses and Aaron, expressing the often-repeated notion that they would have been better off back in Egypt.

God's Answer

In desperation Moses turned to the Lord for answers. This is what he was told, "Take the rod, and gather thou the assembly together, thou, and Aaron thy brother, and *speak ye unto the rock* before their eyes; and it shall give forth his water, and thou shalt bring forth to them water out of the rock" (20:8, italics mine).

Moses Disobeys God

As God had directed, the assembly of Israel gathered together. Our writer now tells us that Moses "with his rod . . . *smote* the rock twice: and the water came out abundantly" (20:11, italics mine). In acting as he did in this scene, we learn that Moses had disobeyed the Lord and was guilty of sin (20:12). Because of the conflict, the spring was called "the water of Meribah," meaning "water of strife" (20:13).

What was Moses' sin? We're only given hints in our lesson. When Moses called the people "rebels" (20:10), the words seem to have had an angry ring. And, while God had told him to "speak" to the rock, we read that he struck the rock twice with his rod. He had disobeyed God's instructions—and quite likely in a rage. The Psalmist seems to validate this idea as he attributes anger to Moses' downfall "at the waters of strife" (Psa. 106:32).

Anger? Lack of faith? Whatever the explanation, we're told that Moses had disobeyed, and the Lord told him that neither he nor his brother could enter the Promised Land. Yes, he had been faithful through many trying circumstances, but he failed this time and the consequence would keep him from realizing his dream.

Paul Applies the Story

In giving a solemn warning to the Christians in Corinth, Paul rehearses this tragic story (1 Cor. 10:4–14), warning his readers against following Israel's bad example. And included in that warning are these words, "Let him that thinketh he standeth take heed lest he fall" (10:12).

Our journey of faith as Christians is often compared to the journey of the children of Israel toward Canaan. Like them, we will experience hard and trying times. Like them, we will confront questions whose answers are veiled at the moment. There may well be those times when circumstances seem stacked against us and God appears to be silent. But in such moments, instead of rebelling and complaining, we are to press steadily on in the confidence of Paul's words when he wrote that "in all these things we are more than conquerors through him [Christ] that loved us" (Rom. 8:37).

Savior, I'm so glad I can trust Your Word—press on steadily, not rebel or complain—but keep confident in You, in spite of what I may be going through. AMEN.

111

WHAT THIS SCRIPTURE MEANS TO ME
Numbers 10:11—20:13

In our lesson, the Israelites approach the Promised Land and send out spies to survey the situation. As I reread the material this time, I found myself understanding the Israelites' fear at the spies' report. A land of giants! A land that devours its inhabitants! It's no wonder they wanted to turn back.

I remember the first teaching job I took, straight out of college. At first, in May, I was very excited. Then, as September grew nearer, I began to be apprehensive about it. Could I do the job? Did I know enough to teach high school students? Could I maintain order in the classroom?

During the August teacher in-service week I began to regret taking the job. I wished I could go back to college. In my mind the students had grown to the size of giants, and I was sure they would devour me on sight the first day of class. I had spent years preparing for this goal. But the closer I came to reaching it, the more frightened I became. Just because I didn't bolt and run like the Israelites doesn't mean I didn't feel like it!

Simon and Garfunkel used to sing a song describing this tendency, saying that the closer we get to a destination, the more we tend to slip-slide away from it. Psychologists call it the approach/avoidance conflict. The Israelites' fear was an early example of something most of us experience at some point in our lives.

What, then, can this lesson show us? For me, it reveals several things.

First of all, it shows us that God is more powerful than we give Him credit for, and He is worthy of more trust than we give Him. Often, by my own assessment, things look impossible and I'm tempted to give up. Yet time and time again, as in the case of my first teaching job, God gives me the strength and the tools to conquer my fear and do the job. If the Israelites had followed Joshua and Caleb and trusted God, they would have conquered the giants.

Also, this lesson shows us in no uncertain terms that disobedience brings consequences. When I was a teenager, taking the car without permission meant getting grounded. Though at the time, the punishment seemed very strict—especially if I thought I had a good reason for taking the car—in the long run, the consequences of disobedience shaped my character and taught me responsibility and trust.

By the same token, the Israelites needed to learn trust and responsibility. Their fear and disobedience was a serious thing. They needed to learn to trust God under all circumstances.

As they found out, running away didn't bring safety or relief from fear. They were out of synch with God's will, and their sin and disobedience brought death in the wilderness.

On a more comforting note, the third thing this lesson shows us is that no matter how rebellious we are as His children, God does not abandon us. God's mercy always shows itself in the end. The Israelites were punished, but not permanently. The next generation would be the inheritors of the Promised Land.

No matter what kind of mess we make of things through fear and disobedience, God can redeem some aspect of it through His power and love.

Even though they became afraid and disobeyed Him, God loved His children over three thousand years ago—and He loves us today. For me, the most powerful message in this lesson is the reminder that God, if we trust Him, will always bring good out of evil.

LESSON 5
Numbers 20:14–36:13

Ready for the Promised Land!

Lord God, As I journey through life, help me keep things in true perspective, always with my eyes focused on the hope of eternal life and the home You have promised. AMEN.

In this, our final study in the Book of Numbers, we look at the last stages of Israel's preparation for their entry into Canaan, the Promised Land. As we have seen, the people have been moving about the wilderness for almost forty years. The most common theme of their experience has been murmuring and complaining, growing out of their regular lapses of faith in God.

While we concluded Lesson 4 with the sad experience at Meribah (20:13), the third major division of the Book of Numbers really comes after Chapter 21. I have chosen, though, to use the section from 20:14–21:35 as an introduction to the final section (22–36). By doing it this way the final events of the Hebrews' wilderness wanderings will be seen in relationship to their encampment in Moab, across from Jericho, and in the light of their final instructions and preparations for entering the Promised Land.

As you read and ponder this last section of Numbers, continue to think of your own life as a journey through the wilderness, struggling with the issues of faith and doubt, obedience and disobedience, hope and despair. Think of life as a journey toward a land that God has promised, a journey often difficult and trying, toward a hope always bright and promising, the hope of life eternal. Far from leading to illusion or escapism, this view enables us to take on the hurts and struggles of the wilderness with strength and fidelity.

The "Exodus" from Kadesh (20:14–29)
Edom's Hostility

Many years before, the people of Israel had refused to invade Canaan from the south because of the negative report of ten of the spies. Now, once again they are poised at Kadesh-barnea for the long-looked-for invasion. This time, though, Moses decides to go east and then north around the southern end of the Dead Sea and on up east of the Jordan River.

So, our Scripture lesson opens with Moses requesting permission to cross the territory of Edom (20:14–17). Requesting permission from the king of Edom was proper and logical, especially since the Hebrews considered the Edomites as kinsmen (20:14). You may remember that Jacob, the "father" of Israel, and Esau, the "father" of Edom, were brothers (Gen. 25:19–26; 33:1–11).

In spite of the fact that Moses' request was reasonable, passage was refused (20:18–21). The refusal carried the threat of war if the Hebrews ventured into Edom. Moses chose not to engage the Edomites in combat, but instead we read that they "journeyed from Kadesh and came unto Mount Hor" (20:22). The location of Mount Hor is not known, but it is significant to our story because it was there that Aaron died (20:23–29).

The Death of Aaron

The Numbers writer tells us that the Lord told Moses to take his brother Aaron and his nephew Eleazar up with him on Mount Hor where Aaron, who had shared in Moses' joys and sorrows for over forty years, would be "gathered unto his people." As

A view of the wilderness area in ancient Edom near the traditional Moses spring. According to tradition it is in this area where Aaron died and was buried.

with Moses, Aaron was not to enter the Promised Land.

What an amazing story of faith this is! There is no record here of complaints or murmuring, no protests or bitterness—only quiet, valiant commitment to follow God's instructions. It was there on the slopes of Mount Hor that Aaron died, and his high priestly garments were put on his son Eleazar who was to be his successor (20:28).

After Aaron died, Moses and Eleazar went back down the mountain and announced the death of Aaron. With this word the people of Israel mourned Aaron's death for thirty days. We're given no hint as to Moses' feelings, but this must have been a sad time for him. Earlier he had lost his sister Miriam. Now his close ally and brother was dead. Humanly speaking, he was probably more alone than ever be-

Near the border between ancient Edom and Moab. Herds of camels can still be seen in this area.

fore, but he also knew that his work wasn't yet finished.

There has long been speculation as to the precise route the Hebrews took from Mount Hor to the point east of the Jordan River from which they would enter Canaan. There were several possible routes, but the likely route, as indicated in this part of our Scripture lesson, has them traveling south and east to Ezion-Geber at the head of the Gulf of Akaba. This would have taken them through the dreadful Wilderness of Paran.

From Ezion-Geber the Hebrews may then have headed north and east of the Dead Sea—a rugged journey of more than one hundred miles through difficult mountainous terrain—and then camped at

The Final Part of the Journey (Chapter 21)
The Probable Route from Mount Hor

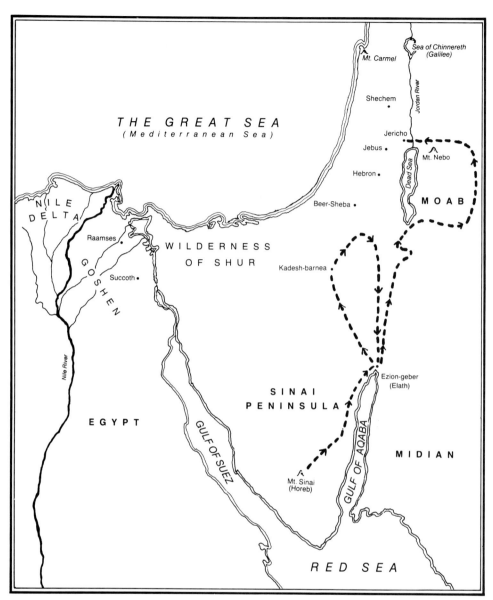

While it is impossible to know for certain the precise route the children of Israel took from Mount Sinai, it is believed they likely headed northeast to the northern tip of the Gulf of Aqaba. From there they probably headed northwest to Kadesh-barnea. It was there the spies were sent into Canaan, and it was to there they returned with their negative report. After the abortive attempt to move into Canaan, contrary to the Lord's instructions to turn back because of their disobedience, they made the wilderness their home for the next thirty-eight years or so. Then to avoid hostile tribes it is thought they may have gone as far south as Ezion-geber before turning north and east again. The route shows them skirting Moab itself and moving into position east of the Jordan River opposite the Canaanite city of Jericho.

the Arnon River. Since the land north of the Arnon was controlled by Sihon, king of the Amorites, Moses sent messengers to him requesting permission to pass through (21:21–22). Not only did Sihon reject Moses' request, but he launched an attack against the Hebrews.

The Numbers writer then tells us that the army of the Hebrews completely defeated Sihon and occupied the land as far north as the Jabbok River (21:23–30). The area north of the Jabbok was controlled by Og, king of Bashon. The Hebrews next engaged Og's armies in battle and defeated them (21:31–35). With this victory, they were in control of all the territory east of the Jordan River except Moab and Edom.

The Brass Serpent

Because of the reference Jesus made to "the serpent in the wilderness," the story found in verses 4–9 of this chapter is of special interest to us. This is the last of the "murmuring stories" the Numbers writer gives us. It is true that the trip from Mount Hor had been a long and hard one, but, as we've seen, the Hebrews had short memories and were master complainers. We read in verse 4 that they were discouraged, and then follow familiar words, "And the people spake against God, and against Moses, Wherefore have ye brought us up out of Egypt to die in the wilderness? for there is no bread, neither is there any water; and our soul loatheth this light bread" (21:5).

In response to their complaining and rebellion we next read that "the Lord sent fiery serpents among the people" (21:6). The snakes that attacked them were quite likely cobras, which are common to that area. Cobra bites are painful and the resulting inflammation would feel like a searing fire.

Once again the people realized that they had sinned against God and asked Moses to pray for them. In response to Moses' prayer, the Lord said, "Make thee a fiery serpent, and set it upon a pole: and it shall come to pass, that every one that is bitten, when he looketh upon it shall live" (21:8). Moses did as he was told and relief came.

We shouldn't look upon this brass snake scene as

some kind of a magical exhibition. Rather, the brass serpent on the pole was a symbol of God's power to help and to heal. Once again, we have seen a patient God responding to the bitter complaining of His people with grace and mercy.

Jesus used this ancient story as a symbol of the ultimate meaning of His own redemptive living and dying. As a look at the brass serpent on the pole provided healing for people in the wilderness, so Jesus presented Himself as the One who, lifted up on the cross, was God's provision for salvation and eternal life (John 3:14–15).

A view of the Arnon gorge. It was from this area that Moses sent messengers to Sihon, king of the Amorites, requesting permission to pass through the territory.

As we move into the concluding chapters of the Book of Numbers, we confront several seemingly unrelated stories and regulations. The first of these—the Balaam story—seems difficult to understand and contradictory at times. Throughout the Bible story he appears to be viewed through different sets of lenses, creating wide speculation among Bible students. Here we will look at Balaam in terms of the present story.

The setting for this part of our story is the plains of Moab on the east side of Jordan across from the ancient city of Jericho (22:1). Balak, the king of the Moabites, had heard of the sweeping victories of the Hebrew army and was afraid (22:2–4).

Then the Numbers writer tells us that Balak sent messengers to a man named Balaam who lived in the distant Euphrates Valley. His reputation as a prophet or seer or wizard was evidently widely known throughout the ancient Near East (22:5).

For reasons not stated Balak believed that whoever Balaam blessed was blessed and whoever he cursed was cursed (22:6). So he asked Balaam to come and curse the threatening Hebrew horde. When Balak's emissaries arrived at Balaam's home, he was glad to see both them and the gold—"the rewards of divination"—they brought. But he evidently felt some hesitation in making an immediate response because he told them, "Lodge here this night, and I will bring you word again, as the Lord shall speak unto me" (22:8).

After waiting through the night for guidance Balaam told the messengers from Moab that God had refused him permission to go with them. The messengers returned home, but when Balak received this report, he sent a larger delegation to put more pressure on Balaam, offering him honor and even more handsome rewards (22:15–17).

Once again Balaam said he would need word from the Lord, and again he suggested they wait until the next day. From the previous word Balaam had re-

The Balaam Saga
(Chapters 22–24)

The Invitation and Balaam's Answer

ceived from the Lord, there seems no reason for him to expect a different answer. Is it possible that because of the size of the financial reward offered, Balaam was hoping God would reverse His thinking? Was this what Balaam was hoping for?

Balaam Leaves for Moab

Obviously, we don't know the answers to such questions. However, it would appear that God did give Balaam permission to go, but only if he said what God told him to say. So next we see him riding his donkey, accompanied by his two servants on his way to Moab with Balak's men.

Then comes an amazing scene, that has long caused widespread speculation. We've tended to get bogged down on the fact that Balaam and his donkey had a conversation with each other. But the important word for the first readers of Numbers and for us is that God has unlimited ways of getting His word across to His people.

According to the writer of the story, three times on the trail the donkey saw the angel of the Lord blocking her path and she shied away. Each time Balaam beat her. Finally, after the third time, we read that "the Lord opened the mouth of the ass," and she chided Balaam for beating her. Then follows one of the strangest conversations in our Bible story (22:28–30). While this was happening, we read that the Lord opened Balaam's eyes, and he saw what the donkey had seen. With that, Balaam offers to return home but is directed by God to continue the mission. However, Balaam is made to understand again that he is to say only what the Lord gives him to say (22:32–35).

The Hebrews would have enjoyed and been amused by this part of the Balaam story. The idea that a donkey appeared to have greater powers than Balaam would have provided some comic relief.

Balaam and Balak Meet

When Balak and Balaam meet, the Mesopotamian seer is upbraided for not coming immediately. Balak seems intent on strutting his ego before Balaam, and he makes it clear he now wants the seer to do what was expected. But Balaam replies simply, "The word that God putteth into my mouth, that shall I speak" (22:38).

Then follows a bit of stage setting as Balaam gives Balak instructions for building altars and offering sacrifices in preparation for receiving word from the Lord (23:1–3). The full meaning of the ritual Balaam called for seems to escape our twentieth-century understanding. But we do know that when he went to the Lord, "God met Balaam" and told him that the time had come to return to Balak and speak the words He gave him (23:4–5). Then beginning with Chapter 23:7 and continuing throughout Chapter 24 we have the record of the four oracles or prophecies that Balaam gave under the leading of God's Spirit.

In the first oracle (23:7–10) Balaam rehearses the fact that Balak had brought him to Moab to curse his Israelite foes, but then he says, "How shall I curse, whom God hath not cursed? or how shall I defy [denounce], whom the Lord hath not defied [denounced]?" (23:8). I'm sure Balaam was amazed at the words the Lord had put into his mouth, and Balak was outraged, "What hast thou done unto me? I took thee to curse mine enemies, and, behold, thou hast blest them altogether" (23:11).

Thinking that a different setting might make things right, Balak moved the action to another place—Mount Pisgah. Here once again they went through the rituals with the altars and the sacrifices. In this new location Balaam consulted with the Lord again (23:13–16).

With the stage properly set, Balaam opened his mouth and Balak heard the second oracle or prophecy after a suitable introduction, "Behold, I have received commandment to bless: and he hath blessed; and I cannot reverse it" (23:20). In other words, the Hebrews were blest by God; He found no fault with them. He was their God and they were His people. The change of location and setting hadn't affected the will of the Lord. It never does. God's promises— His agreements—can be counted on!

The Four Oracles or Prophecies

With Balaam's second word from the Lord, Balak was getting desperate. In effect, he told Balaam neither to bless nor to curse the Hebrews (23:25).

Once more Balak shifts the scene of action "unto the top of Peor." From this high point they were able to see the entire camp of the Hebrews. Here again they went through the ritual of the altars and sacrifices. Then we read that the Spirit of the Lord came upon Balaam as he reviewed the way the Lord had blessed Israel (24:1–8). And following that review Balaam said, "Blessed is he that blesseth thee, and cursed is he that curseth thee" (24:9).

When Balak heard that third prophecy he was outraged. He berated Balaam and told him to leave immediately. And with that, came the fourth of Balaam's prophecies in which he predicts the final destruction of the Moabites (24:15–19). The story then ends with a masterful understatement, "And Balaam rose up, and went and returned to his place: and Balak also went his way" (24:25).

It is interesting that throughout this whole scenario the Hebrews were completely oblivious to what was going on. But when the word reached them, they must have been greatly relieved and encouraged. Here was another affirmation that God was with them. Positioned as they were on the east side of the Jordan with the Canaan campaign ahead, this must have been good news.

The message of this complex scene for us is that our God can be depended on. He will keep His promises. We can count on Him. Balaam, for all the complexities of his nature and background, was not for sale and could not be corrupted.

**Tragedy at Shittim
(Chapter 25)**

In this part of our Scripture lesson we have two tragic stories. The first is about widespread sexual immorality with Moabite women, and the second has to do with an illicit relationship or marriage with a Midianite woman.

*The Wrong Women and
False Gods*

Shittim in Hebrew means "the Acacia," and was a site east of Jericho and the Jordan River. It was Israel's last camp before their invasion of the Promised

Land. The name itself suggests a shady and delightful setting, a place where the men of Israel could become relaxed and less than vigilant. Within a short time we're told the men became enamored with some of the local women—a not uncommon happening in the annals of military history.

With sexual relations came acceptance of and involvement in some of the religious rituals of the Moab women (25:1–5). And to participate in the worship of a god, to Israel, was to declare oneself as a follower of that god, a serious and punishable transgression of the Covenant between God and His people. Central to the fidelity of Israel to the Covenant was the rejection of all other gods.

As they had begun their journey worshiping the Golden Calf at Sinai, so they conclude their journey from Sinai worshiping the Baal of Peor. What happened at Shittim is a dark forecast of what will happen again and again once they have occupied Canaan. The pagan cults of the Baals were everywhere to be found among the Canaanites, and Israel's perpetual absorption of the local religions became the continuing tragedy of their history.

And the pattern continues today! How much the church in the Western world has absorbed the cultural religion of affluence and success. It's not always easy to differentiate between being "a good Christian" and being a good citizen of Western democracies. Sometimes the two may fit well. But we must remain aware that the gods of this world may indeed blind our eyes to the God of Abraham, Isaac, and Jacob, the God of Moses, and the God and Father of our Lord Jesus Christ.

As the second story begins, the people are already suffering from a plague, perhaps as a result of the previous incident or from some other judgment of God upon them (25:6–18). The people are assembled in front of the Tabernacle.

In the middle of this desperate plague setting a Hebrew named Zimri brought a Midianite woman named Cozbi into the camp. It is not clear whether or not he had married her, but even if he had, a

Zimri and the Midianite Woman

marriage with a pagan Midianite was not permitted. The corruption of their faith through intermarriage with people who worshiped other gods was a constant source of trouble for the children of Israel.

The Zeal of Phinehas Is Rewarded

While the zealous action of Phinehas may seem to us like an uncontrolled act of violence, to them this was a matter of life or death, since many people had already died as a result of such flagrant violations of the Covenant (25:7–9). The zeal for fidelity demonstrated by Phinehas stopped the plague, and he was honored by God by being named successor to Eleazar, his father, as high priest.

From our vantage point in time, the action taken by Phinehas and other Old Testament characters may seem extreme and barbarous. It is very easy for us to call those ancient people primitive. But, unfortunately, the pages of modern history in twentieth-century Europe, in Korea, in Vietnam, in Central America, and certain Third World countries are stained by actions equally as ruthless and cruel. But there is a difference. We've had almost two thousand years of Christian history as a compass for our faith and actions. Our spiritual ancestors camped east of the Jordan—God's covenant people—had rigorous lessons still to learn. To sin against the commandment of God produced dire consequences then and now.

A New Generation (Chapters 26–27)
A Second Census

As the Hebrews had taken a count of all of the ablebodied males over twenty years of age prior to leaving Sinai, so now, almost forty years later, upon instructions from the Lord, another count is taken (Chapter 26). This second census highlights the fact that a new generation now filled the ranks. Virtually all of those who had left Egypt had passed on (26:63–65).

God Is Still Active in His World

A review of the figures given here and those recorded in the first census indicates that while the size of certain tribes has increased, the overall totals are somewhat less. Of significance to us is the reality that though individuals lived and died, and the size of some tribes had changed, the action of God continued through His people—even as it still does.

There's a source of strength in the thought that you and I are a part of this continuing redemptive drama of God's action in the world. We may not live to see the realization of our hopes and dreams for God's Kingdom—His new society—on earth, but we mustn't lose sight of our participation in the eternal drama of God's salvation. As the writer of the Book of Hebrews expressed it, "Wherefore seeing we also are compassed about [surrounded by] with so great a cloud of witnesses, let us lay aside every weight, and . . . run with patience the race that is set before us, Looking unto Jesus, the author and finisher of our faith" (Heb. 12:1–2).

The Case of the Family of Zelophehad

The second census, especially relating to the division of land among the tribes and clans, raised a special problem in the case of the family of Zeloph-

A view of ancient Gilead, an area east of the Jordan River and north of Moab. This was part of the area settled by Reuben, Gad, and the half tribe of Manasseh.

ehad. He was a member of the tribe of Manasseh who had five daughters but no sons (27:1–11).

Those of us whose children are all female can identify with him to some degree, but not entirely. For, you see, in ancient Israel, daughters could not receive a share of a father's inheritance. And this meant that they would have no property in the Promised Land. The case was brought to the Lord by Moses and settled in favor of the daughter. The ruling was clear; in such a situation, where there were no sons, a father's inheritance passed first to his daughters, or to his brothers, or to the nearest kinsman.

To those of us who have been shaped by the ideal in which there is neither male nor female in Christ (Gal. 3:28), the daughters of Zelophehad must be celebrated as pioneers in the long movement toward guaranteeing the rights of women. Their courage in going against the grain of their culture was rewarded and affirmed by God. From that time, daughters as well as sons were to be granted their equal rights in their inheritance among the people of God.

Joshua's Appointment As Leader

The final section of Chapter 27 stands as a towering tribute to the greatness of Moses. As he already knows, he will not be allowed to enter the Promised Land with the people because of his earlier disobedience (Chapter 20).

After his long years of faithful service and leadership, through all of the frustrations and hardships of the wilderness, and now having brought them to the very edge of the Promised Land, he is told to view it and prepare to die (27:12–13).

His first response was a prayer in which he asked God to raise up a special leader for His people so they wouldn't be like "sheep which have no shepherd" (27:17). And then he obediently did as God commanded—he "laid his hands" on Joshua before the assembled Hebrews and commissioned him for his new leadership task (27:22–23).

By his action at this time of his life, Moses modeled for us a very special grace. He graciously accepted the word of the Lord by stepping aside at the right moment and turning the responsibilities of leadership on to the next generation.

The Lord then, through Moses, laid out for His people an orderly plan of worship. This annual cycle of worship festivals was not meant to be a fearsome burden. Rather, it was to be a constant reminder and give needed direction. Our Christian church year has its roots in the carefully detailed instructions given here for the offerings that were to be made in the exercise of worship.

The Church Year (Chapters 28–29)

First, instructions are given for those offerings of worship that were to be made every day—burnt offerings, a cereal (meat) offering, and a drink offering (28:3–8). These were a most important part of Israel's worship. The practice of daily worship has long been seen as essential to spiritual health and to a vital walk with God. For us, the equivalent of the daily offerings the Hebrews were to make is the daily practice of reading, reflection, prayer, and praise.

The Daily Offerings

Next came those offerings and acts of worship that were to be made on the Sabbath Day (28:9–10). While for the Hebrews, every day was to be lived for the Lord, one day in seven—the Sabbath—was holy. And on the Sabbath their daily offerings were to be doubled. Observing the Sabbath had long been a part of Hebrew life, but here now for the first time we find mention of specific offerings to be made.

For the Christian, Sabbath worship is equally important for spiritual health. Our Sabbath, the first day of the week, Sunday, is not merely a day of rest. It is a time of worship. It is a time when we commemorate the resurrection of Jesus on that first Easter morning.

The Sabbath Offerings

At the beginning of each month, special offerings, acts of worship, were to be made. In addition to the regular burnt offering of two young bulls, a ram, seven lambs, the cereal and drink offerings, a young goat was added as a sin offering. This ritual of wor-

The New Moon Offerings

ship was to be announced by the blowing of the silver trumpets (10:10). The first day of the month was a time of celebration.

The Passover and the Feast of Unleavened Bread

This special festival was celebrated for one week every year (28:16–25). It commemorated the Hebrews' deliverance from Egyptian slavery and the beginning of their new life as the people of God. This festival was observed in the spring of the year in the Hebrew month of Nisan—our April or May.

For us as Christians, the Apostle Paul points out that Christ became our Passover offering (1 Cor. 5:7–8).

The Feast of Weeks

In Exodus 23:16 the Feast of Weeks is referred to as the Feast of Harvest. It was a special day set aside to celebrate the beginning of the harvest (28:26–31). This celebration was held during the Hebrew month Iyyar or Ziw, the equivalent of May or June. At this time the firstfruits of the harvest were brought as an offering to God.

The Feast of Trumpets

In addition to the regular monthly celebrations, the Feast of Trumpets was celebrated at the beginning of the seventh month (29:1–6). The number seven represented God's completed creation—a number of special significance to the Hebrews.

The Day of Atonement

Ten days after the Feast of the Trumpets the Day of Atonement was joyously and solemnly observed (29:7–11). You may find it helpful to stop a moment and review our discussion of Leviticus 16. This was the one day the high priest entered the Holy of Holies and the day the scapegoat was driven out into the wilderness carrying the sins of the people.

The Feast of Tabernacles

This was perhaps the happiest festival of the Jewish year and came just five days after the Day of Atonement (29:12–40). During this celebration the people lived in booths in memory of their life in the wilderness. Also called the Feast of Ingathering, this celebration occurred during our months of September or October. It was a time of thanksgiving and joy as the harvest was completed. This festival continues to be a vital part of Jewish life and worship.

The Christian Message

It would be very easy to pass quickly over the description of these ancient forms of worship—or we might even ignore them entirely—but it seems to me this would be to lose something important.

Because of the frequent references even in the New Testament to the ancient Hebrew forms of worship it is helpful for us to be familiar with them. However, of equal importance is the recognition of the care God seemed to be taking to organize and structure the worship patterns of His people. Each of the feasts or festivals were related to the actions of God in behalf of His people and served as regular and constant reminders of the marvelous provisions of His grace.

The offering of these sacrifices and the celebration of the festival occasions were not to be followed as superficial or surface acts. Rather, the deep meaning of each one gave intensity and urgency and richness to a person's devotional life. In similar fashion, many people are being enriched in their devotional lives today by celebrating each day and season that marks and gives meaning to the Christian year. The word that God impressed upon our spiritual ancestors at Sinai and in their camp in Moab as to the importance of regular worship seems increasingly applicable in the hurly-burly of our late-twentieth-century life.

The Law Regarding Vows (Chapter 30)
The Seriousness of Making Vows

The thrust of this particular part of our Scripture lesson was to impress the reader of the seriousness with which vows were taken. Great care is taken in these instructions that both men and women regard their vows as sacred. A person's word, once given, was to be kept. I suggest that after you have read Chapter 30, you go back and read Leviticus 27.

There were basically two kinds of vows that were made: (1) those that promise to give something to God; (2) those that promise to abstain from doing something for a period of time.

Vows Made by Women

Most of this chapter is devoted to vows that were taken by women (30:3–16). Four distinct types of situations are mentioned here: vows taken by an unmarried woman who lives in her father's home; a woman who was single at the time she made her vow but who got married before fulfilling the terms of the vow; vows taken by widows or divorced women; and vows taken by a married woman.

The specific situations described in this ancient setting are quite foreign to us, but each carried important implication in the life and culture of ancient Israel. The counterpart of these for us is found in our marriage vows and our vows of baptism, church membership, and of specialized service, either by clergy or lay persons, in the work of the Lord. The important word for us here comes in the reminder that the promises—the vows—we make to God and to each other are sacred and are to be kept.

The War with the Midianites (Chapter 31)

The Numbers writer now directs our attention to a rather difficult and gory scene. You will recall that in the closing verses of Chapter 25 mention was made of an encounter with the Midianites because of what happened at Peor. Now we are introduced to a full-scale battle.

You will recall also that Midian was a son of Abraham and Keturah. His descendants peopled the desert area north of the Arabian peninsula and along the eastern frontier of Palestine. Moses' father-in-law was a Midianite. Relations between the Midianites and the children of Israel ran hot and cold over the years—sometimes friendly and sometimes not. They were apparently a wealthy Arab nation.

As a result of the incident mentioned in Chapter 25, the Midianites at this time were regarded as enemies. Their attempts at corrupting the morals of the Hebrews and their efforts at trying to influence them to idolatrous worship apparently had to be dealt with. A holy war was declared out of what was regarded as a religious and moral necessity.

While the carnage pictured here is vivid, the real

focus of the story is that God's will and purposes cannot be thwarted without grave consequences of one kind or another. While different circumstances over the centuries call for varied responses, we know that in all situations the God of the Bible is active in history. His purposes will be accomplished.

Settling East of the Jordan River (Chapter 32)

When all of the area in Transjordan—east of the Jordan river—was in the hands of the Hebrews, it became obvious that the moment of the Canaan invasion was close. The Transjordan country was exceptionally fertile. The tribes of Reuben and Gad requested permission to settle in this area because of their large herds of cattle.

When Moses heard their request, he was indignant. He accused them of wanting to desert their compatriots and avoid the war of Canaan conquest. And with his accusations he rehearsed a bit of history (32:6–15). Then came a counteroffer. The men of Reuben and Gad would get their families settled and then go with their brothers and help them conquer Canaan (32:16–19). This was agreeable. Moses gave his permission and the settling process began (32:20–38).

A portion of the tribe of Manasseh requested permission to also locate east of the Jordan. It was granted, and they settled to the north of Reuben and Gad (32:39–42). And as we will see in a future study, the men of Reuben and Gad and Manasseh whose families settled east of the Jordan were faithful to their promise and fought side by side with their fellow Hebrews until the land was conquered.

From Egypt to Canaan (Chapter 33)

Because of the people's disobedience, the trip from Egypt to Canaan had stretched out to some forty years. Now, in this chapter we have a rehearsal of the itinerary they had followed (33:1–49). The Numbers writer credits Moses as the author (1:2). It is believed this section was written to be read aloud because of its exceptional rhythm.

Of the forty-two encampments mentioned here, eighteen appear nowhere else. Few of the places can be located with certainty. But this listing was not intended as an itinerary to be traced like a tour trip. Instead, it was a witness to a pilgrimage made by a group of people in which God had been faithful at all points. The author was not writing geography or history; he was recording God's actions in behalf of His people.

In the closing verses of this chapter (23:50–56) the Hebrews are reminded of the necessity of obedience to the will of God as a condition for settling the Land of Promise—they are to conquer all of the people and destroy everything associated with the worship of the Canaanite pagan gods. Nothing of Canaanite culture or religion is to find its way into their life-style.

The New Testament counterpart to this complete separation from the ways of the world is expressed by Paul to the Corinthian Christians and to us, "Wherefore come out from among them, and be ye separate, saith the Lord, and touch not the unclean thing; and I will receive you, And will be a Father unto you, and ye shall be my sons and daughters, saith the Lord Almighty" (2 Cor. 6:17–18).

**Tribal Boundaries
(Chapter 34)**

It's obviously getting close to D-Day, for Moses now gives instructions as to the boundaries and the allotment of the land to each tribe after Canaan has been subjugated. This would be done by lot among the nine and a half tribes settling across the Jordan, since Gad, Reuben, and half the tribe of Manasseh had chosen to occupy land on the east side of the river.

Apart from Caleb, the ten leaders appointed to handle the distribution of the land are unknown. Of the twelve scouts sent out by Moses from Kadesh-Barnea, only Joshua and Caleb are left. In each case, the meanings of their names have clear significance: Shemuel, Name of God; Elidad, My God loves; Bukki, Proved; Hanniel, Grace of God; Kemuel, Raised by God; Elizaphan, My God protects; Paltiel, God is my deliverance; Ahihud, My brother is magnificent; and Pedahel, God delivers.

To believe that God gives each of us a name, a gift by which we may serve him, is essential to self-knowledge and proper self-love.

Cities for the Levites (Chapter 35)

After the instructions were given for the allotment of land among the tribes, it became necessary to make provision for the Levites who, because of their priestly duties, would not be involved in the conquering process. Consequently, the Lord makes it clear through Moses that forty-eight cities are to be established among the tribes for the Levites. We further learn here that six of these cities are to be designated as cities of refuge. Cities of refuge were to be havens for persons who had killed someone without intending to do so and without premeditation.

Put simply, if a person by accident or without premeditation killed another person, he could escape to a city of refuge and thereby escape the vengeance of the dead person's nearest of kin who had the right in those days to avenge the murder of a relative. The fugitive would be given a trial by the elders of the city of refuge, and if they found that he was not guilty of premeditated murder, he would be given asylum—his safety was assured. He could remain in that city, but was, in a sense, an exile.

There is no specifically Christian application of the idea of cities of refuge. However, we are assured refuge from the penalty of sin by virtue of Christ's death and resurrection and our acceptance of Him as Savior and Lord.

Tribal Marriage Restrictions (Chapter 36)

Now, in this final scene in the Book of Numbers the daughters of Zelophehad (27:1–11) are back in the limelight, and for good reason. A complication had arisen on the problem of allotment of land in Canaan by inheritance. For example, if a daughter married outside of her tribe, her property would go with her to the other tribe. This would not only cause endless confusion but would violate the original allotment made to each tribe.

For this reason, Moses ruled that each of the daughters of Zelophehad could marry only within the tribe of Manasseh—their own tribe. This established a precedence that secured the original tribal divisions.

The Book of Numbers
for Today

In a sense it seems that the Book of Numbers ends on sort of an anticlimactic note. There's no grand finale. But what we have had is a collection of details essential in the final preparation for the Hebrew people—the sons of Jacob—for entry into their Land of Promise. They were about to claim their inheritance under God as first promised to the Patriarch Abraham.

But when we reflect on the saga of this unusual and often neglected book, we do find an application to our twentieth-century Christian pilgrimage. The Hebrews, the children of Israel, had been on a long and arduous journey, even as we are. We see that strength and endurance for the journey come by keeping our eyes firmly fixed on the glory of our ultimate destination.

All of this reminds me of a lecture I heard the late D. T. Niles of Ceylon give at Princeton Theological Seminary. In this lecture he described his journey. From his home in Ceylon, he walked two miles down a stony path. He then mounted a donkey and rode to the bus station where he got a bus that took him to the airport. And at the airport he caught the first of several flights that would eventually get him to New York City.

Then flashing back to the beginning of his trip in rural Ceylon, he told us that on the first leg of that journey he had stumbled over a rock on the path. Since he was wearing open sandals his toe was badly injured. Then he grinned as he told us that under normal circumstances, instead of going on when he was hurt, he would have limped back home for treatment and sympathy. But because of the importance of the trip and of his destination he continued on in spite of the pain.

This is indeed a modern parable of what happened in the wilderness of Sinai and the trek to the invasion point east of the Jordan. It was the glory of their destination that kept them going in spite of the hardships and reverses.

For us, the pain of the journey cannot be compared

with the joy of walking with the Lord and serving Him in the here and now—even as we press ahead to that future place that God through Christ has prepared for us.

"The sufferings of this present time are not worthy to be compared with the glory which shall be revealed in us." Thank You, Father, for the joy of walking with You! AMEN.

WHAT THIS SCRIPTURE MEANS TO ME
Numbers 20:14—36:13

This lesson is action-packed! These seventeen chapters cover many, many incidents and events during the Israelites' remaining years in the desert. Aaron dies, the Israelites fight several nations and win, new rules are added and offerings made, God gives instructions for the conquest of Canaan, and some of the tribes settle east of the Jordon.

Among all the stories and events recorded in our lesson, I am captivated and bothered most by the story of Balaam. That sly fox personifies to an extreme degree one of my own characteristics that I don't like very well— the desire to have my cake and eat it too.

I remember as a child being torn between wanting to be a good little girl and come inside when I was called, and wanting to have fun with my friends. How long could I stay outside and play before I made my mother really angry?

As an adult, too, I am faced with similar dilemmas. For instance, I want to be a good steward of the money God has given me by donating to the church and worthwhile charities. But at the same time, I want to buy extra things for myself and my family. I am pulled between tithing and keeping the money. I want to do both.

Balaam also suffered from contradictory desires. He wanted to obey God and do the right thing, but he also wanted the money Balak offered him if he would curse the Israelites.

At first Balaam resisted the temptation to disobey God. Then bit by bit he succumbed, always trying to stay on God's good side. Though Balaam ostensibly followed God's will by not cursing the Israelites outright, in the end he did give some advice that created serious problems. He advised the king not to attack them, but to corrupt them from within. By this method, he almost got to have it both ways.

Balaam reminds me of a shrewd politician. I worked for a year and a half in Washington, D.C., and I sometimes heard stories of government officials who wanted both a perfectly clean public record and large sums of money available through questionable means. They would go to great lengths of self-deception and public rationalization; but many of them—like Balaam—got caught eventually with their hands in the till.

When we become devious and try to take matters out of God's hand into our own, we get into trouble. We may think, "It's all right to make this slightly shady deal, so long as it's technically legal." Or, in a different context, we may say to ourselves, "It's O.K. to gossip or hold grudges as long as I'm going to church. I'm obeying God by doing good deeds and by being active in the church. Who will notice if I don't speak to Mary Jane?" We may even fool people—including ourselves—into thinking we are doing the right thing. But we can't fool God.

For me, this lesson is a powerful reminder that in matters of faith we cannot have our cake and eat it too. We cannot follow two divergent wills, ours and God's. God demands our total obedience with no compromise. Ideally the two wills—God's and ours—will become one.

Furthermore, if we obey God, we will be blessed. Our blessing may not be money or whatever it is we think we want, but in the long run God's blessing is more fulfilling than anything we could desire on our own.

LESSON 6
Deuteronomy 1–11

The Faithfulness of God

Dear Lord, As Moses spoke Your word to the people long ago, so may his words be Your words to me this day. AMEN.

Welcome to one of the greatest books of the Old Testament! It is quoted more than eighty times in the New Testament and is joined by Genesis, Psalms, and Isaiah as the most often quoted Old Testament books. It is a book which we desparately need to rediscover, for though it is not one of the most widely read books in Christian circles, it has a vital message for our time.

The Lord Jesus apparently had a special love for the Book of Deuteronomy. During His temptation experience in the wilderness, He responded to each taunt of the Tempter with words from it: "Man shall not live by bread alone, but by every word that proceedeth out of the mouth of God"; "Thou shalt not tempt the Lord thy God"; and, "Thou shalt worship the Lord thy God, and Him only shalt thou serve" (Matt. 4:4, 7, 10; quoting from Deut. 8:3, 6:16; 6:13).

Both Judaism and Christianity affirm the central truth of Deuteronomy, that the basic demand of God is to "love the Lord thy God with all thine heart, and with all thy soul, and with all thy might" (Deut. 6:5; Mark 12:28–30). The Book of Deuteronomy has had an immeasurable influence on the faith and life of both Jews and Christians.

In a time when the single greatest need of the church is its renewal, we will do well to turn again to the message of this book. In the year 622 B.C., when Israel's faith was lagging and its institutions were in decay, King Josiah was told that a "book of the law" had been discovered in the Temple (2 Kings 22–23; 2 Chron. 34–35). Upon hearing its contents, Josiah called an assembly of priests, prophets, and the people for the reading of this newly discovered book. This led to a deep repentance and a renewal of the Covenant, followed by significant reforms in both their worship and their common life, culminating in a celebration of the Passover.

I believe that the rediscovery of the essence and power of the Book of Deuteronomy could be a source of renewal today. Now, as then, the world is in the throes of political tension and military engagement. Then, perhaps as now, God called a relatively small community to commit itself completely to Him as an outpost of the kingdom of God—a sign of the kingdom yet to come. Listen for the Word of God as we study this amazing book.

An Overview of the Book

Just as it's a good idea to consult a road map before starting on an unfamiliar journey, it will be good for us to develop an understanding of the basic structure of Deuteronomy before beginning our study. The book is written in the form of a series of addresses by Moses, all delivered within a few days. In Exodus, Leviticus, and Numbers, God is portrayed as speaking to Moses in order to reveal His law and commands for the Hebrew people. In Deuteronomy, Moses is portrayed as speaking to the people in preparing them for their entry into Canaan after the forty years of wandering in the Sinai desert.

For our three studies, we shall group together Chapters 1–11, 12–28, and 29–34. But it is important to recognize that the basic structure of the book is built around three addresses of Moses. The first address is contained in 1:6–4:40. Here we have a recital of what God had done with the people of Israel since the giving of the Law at Mount Sinai, referred to in Deuteronomy as Mount Horeb.

The second address is contained in Chapters 5:1–28:68. This is an extended oration about the importance of allegiance and obedience to God. Moses' third address is contained in Chapters 29 and 30. It is a final appeal of Moses for faithfulness to God. Then in Chapters 31–34 we have the record of some of the last acts of Moses, along with the story of his death. With this basic road map, we now begin our journey.

A Preamble (1:1–5)

While some scholars feel that these opening verses of Deuteronomy are more likely the closing verses of Numbers, they actually serve as a helpful preamble to the Book of Deuteronomy. Before leadership can be transferred from Moses to Joshua and before the conquest of Canaan begins, the Covenant made between God and His people at Sinai must be renewed.

The place names listed in these verses cannot be located with certainty. But the narrative makes it clear that we are dealing with actual places, especially with the reference to the traveling time between Horeb and Kadesh-barnea, a fact now well confirmed. Horeb was the name of the general region in which Mount Sinai was located.

Of extreme importance to our understanding of the Bible is the fact that God makes Himself known to real people in actual places in specific times. The writer of Deuteronomy dates the words of Moses on the first day of the eleventh month of the fortieth year since the giving of the Law at Sinai. This is the only date given in the entire book, and the only one really necessary to establish the setting for all that follows.

It is clear from the outset that Moses spoke only that which had been given to him by God. He was a man under orders. The title of the book, "Deuteronomy," is somewhat misleading, for it means literally, "a second giving of the law." This idea came from the Greek rendering of a phrase in Chapter 17:18 where the king who is to rule over Israel is instructed to prepare "a copy of this law." In the Hebrew Bible Deuteronomy is usually titled, "These are the words," or simply "Words," from the opening words of the Hebrew text. We might more accurately title the book, "A Proclamation of the Covenant."

What we have in Deuteronomy is not the Law being given a second time, but an exposition and application of the Law already given.

Moving Out! (1:6–18)

Moses began his first address with a reminder of the call of God that had come to them after they had been in camp at Mount Sinai for a year. The people were reminded that centuries before, Abraham had received God's promise of his descendants' becoming a special people and occupying a new land. At Sinai God had made the Covenant with them and had given them the Law. And they had also been given the Tabernacle, and a system of worship and sacrifices. Now they are reminded of God's rallying words, "Ye have dwelt long enough in this mount: Turn you, and take your journey" (1:6–7).

Reluctant to Change

At that time forty years earlier, I have to believe these instructions came as a threat and a disruption to those who had grown accustomed to the camp at Sinai. It is quite human to become comfortable with where we are even if it's not where we ought to be. And that is true not just about physical places but equally, if not more so, about the emotional and spiritual places of life.

It seems to me that we need to be reminded constantly that God calls us to be pioneers, not settlers. All too often the seven last words of the church are, "But we've always done it that way!" But resistance to change closes off the possibility of growth. Unfortunately, though, we have an inborn fear of venturing into the unknown. We hold back even when we know deep down that we can't stay where we are.

A view of Moab. It was in a setting like this that Israel was camped during the Deuteronomy story.

This was certainly true of a friend of mine who was wrestling with the problems alcohol was causing in his life and relationships. As we talked, I could see that he was trying to overcome his problems without making any radical changes in his life. We counseled together for several months, but in spite of my urgings he steadfastly refused to get involved with an Alcoholics Anonymous group or enter a program of therapy.

Finally, my friend, after a most fearful incident, agreed to attend an A.A. group if I would go with him. We went, and that was the beginning of a life of sobriety that has continued now for eleven years. This man, like so many of us, had become attached to and comfortable with destructive patterns of relating and behaving. And even though his problems were painful, he had for so long resisted the idea of change. But, "happy are the pioneers who hit the trail at God's calling."

Moses had known, too, that in their preparation for "moving out" the Hebrews needed to be organized and he must have help. As he had come to understand, no leader can do the job alone (1:9). But then, even as now, the success in delegating leadership to others depends on getting quality people (1:13–17).

Organization and the Delegation of Authority

Next, Moses rehearses the tragic events that took place in Kadesh-barnea. I suggest you take a few moments and reread our discussion of Numbers 13 and 14 where we have a longer description of this story.

Unbelief and Defeat (1:19–46)
The Tragedy at Kadesh-barnea

Their journey of about one hundred miles from Mount Sinai to Kadesh had been difficult, but they had managed it. They had set up their base camp at Kadesh-barnea on the southern border of Canaan and were poised and ready to move into the land God had promised Abraham centuries before (1:19–21).

But then came the suggestion of sending spies into Canaan on a reconnoitering mission—an indication in itself of their unbelief in God's faithfulness. When the spies came back and the people of Israel heard the majority report, they became paralyzed with fear and took matters into their own hands. Fear and anxiety were their mortal enemies, and they refused the course God had set for them.

Then when God told them the consequences of their fear and anxiety and unbelief, they stubbornly decided to try an invasion on their own though God now forbad it. But their efforts turned into a rout because God wasn't with them (1:22–45).

Do you agree that their story is our story? God is ever calling us, personally and collectively, to lives of faithful obedience. Jesus calls us to "take up crosses," suffering on behalf of others, sacrificing for the sake of the poor and oppressed, taking unpopular stands for the sake of righteousness. But sometimes in our journey of discipleship we see "the giants," ten feet tall and menacing. Fear then takes over, we back off

Their Story Is Our Story

and take matters and events into our own hands. We try to do things our way and suffer the tragic results of acting without God. Our fear and anxiety produce unbelief.

**Faith and Victory
(2:1–3:11)**
*Thirty-eight Years in a
Nutshell*

As Moses continues to rehearse the passing events in this his first address to the people of Israel, he makes a brief reference to their travels after they turned away from Kadesh-barnea (2:4–23). It was a long, circuitous route, and is described in much more detail in our study of Numbers 20 and 21.

Victory in Transjordan

Moses then moves on to speak of their most recent victories over Sihon, the Amorite king of Heshbon (2:24–37) and Og, the king of Bashon (3:1–11). These latest victories had given the Hebrews the territory north of the Arnon River and east of the Jordan River—a solid military base from which to launch an invasion of Canaan.

Og must have been an imposing giant of a man. One thing is sure—the writer of Deuteronomy was impressed with his size, for he took the space here to include the size of Og's bed. This has to be the fore-runner of our twentieth-century king-sized beds—it measured thirteen feet in length and was six feet wide!

A Theological Reflection

As we read this quick review of Israel's journey, I think it is important that we not put the "newspaper" down without doing some theological reflection. To the children of Israel, events like those Moses is recounting here were always understood in relation to God. Yes, they were concerned with victory or defeat, but they were more deeply interested in what God was doing.

Of tremendous importance to the Hebrews as they heard this part of Moses' address was the reminder that God had neither broken nor forgotten His Covenant with Abraham and his descendants. This was the grand reaffirmation—that God always keeps His word and that they, as Abraham's descendants, were indeed blessed and would have a land of their own.

Another important reminder comes through: God

works His purposes through people who are faithful and obedient to Him. After all, there hadn't been any reason except their own unbelief and lack of faith for them not to have invaded Canaan directly from the south thirty-eight years before.

At the same time, there is a powerful statement here on God's grace and forgiveness. Even though they had been unfaithful those many years ago at Kadesh-barnea, God had remained faithful to them. The marvelous affirmation of that is seen in these words, "For the Lord thy God hath blessed thee in all the works of thy hand: he knoweth thy walking through this great wilderness: these forty years the Lord thy God hath been with thee; thou hast lacked nothing" (2:7).

God Doesn't Give Up on Us

What a joy it is to affirm God's faithfulness to weary and worn pioneers! A middle-aged man came to one of our church conferences with his teen-aged son from whom he had been estranged for years. He had left his wife and children years before. The son had come to a vital relationship with Christ and looked up his father in order to share the good news of God's love. Before the conference was over, the father had begun to experience God's love through loving and caring people. As a result he became active in A.A. and in church membership, and was changed into a sober, active Christian disciple and witness.

Before he was baptized, he said to me, "I still can't believe that God could erase the hell of these last fifteen years, and especially of a lifetime of total disobedience to Him. But I've finally begun to live— by the grace of God!" Because of his dissipation he only lived for two more years, but not long before he died, he said, "I'm so grateful that God didn't give up on me. These past two years have been most beautiful and joyful, and now I will live with Him eternally." Indeed, God is ever gracious, the waiting Father who accepts any and all prodigals who return.

When God Says No (3:12–29)

After describing the division of the land east of the Jordan among the tribes of Reuben and Gad and half

147

of the tribe of Manasseh (3:12–20), the Deuteronomy writer gives us one of the most touching and profound passages in all of the Bible.

Moses' Plea

Moses next reminds his people of his earlier prayer. The pathos in these words is deeply moving, "O Lord God, thou hast begun to shew thy servant thy greatness, and thy mighty hand: for what God is there in heaven or in earth, that can do according to thy works, and according to thy might? I pray thee, *let me go over, and see the good land that is beyond Jordan,* that goodly mountain, and Lebanon" (3:24–25, italics mine). These words reflect the keen disappointment and frustration Moses felt. This became very real to me one day as I stood where Moses had on Pisgah and read these words aloud to a group of fellow travelers.

A Breathtaking View

As we stood that day 2,600 feet above sea level and 4,000 feet above the Dead Sea, the panorama took our breath away. Far to the north and northwest were the peaks of Mount Hermon and Mount Tabor. Then, moving our eyes south, we could make out the peaks of Mount Ebal and Mount Gerizim in Samaria. Looking west we caught sight of the Mount of Olives and the golden skyline of Jerusalem. To the southwest we could make out the hills in which Bethlehem and Hebron lie. Finally, directly below us as we faced west was the mysterious Dead Sea, shimmering under the haze of its perpetual evaporation.

Before us in one sweeping vista was the Land of Promise. We were seeing it just as Moses had after forty years of frustration in the desert wilderness—a "good land." And so he pleaded, "Let me go over."

God's Answer to Moses' Plea

God's answer to Moses was a clear-cut no. All that God would permit was a view of the land from the heights of Pisgah. As I thought about it, this seemed like an unfair answer. After all, he had put up with a lot as the leader of his people. And, for the most part he had been faithful and obedient to God. At that point I think I would have argued with God, but

Moses seemed quietly to have accepted the Lord's decision.

As my fellow travelers and I walked down the slopes of Pisgah that day, I longed to share not only the frustrated anger of Moses but his submission to the will of God as well. And I was reminded of Another who prayed, "Abba, Father, all things are possible unto thee; take away this cup from me: nevertheless not what I will, but what thou wilt" (Mark 14:36). That's the kind of person I want to be—strong enough in my trust to leave things up to God. I want to be able to accept God's nos with the poise and grace of Moses and Jesus.

Having reviewed the history of Israel in which God's faithful love has been central, Moses then made a strong appeal for the people to be faithful in their obedience to God. This emphasis prepared the way for the proclamation of the Ten Commandments and the laws growing out of them.

First Moses set the stage by saying, "Ye shall not add unto the word . . . neither shall ye diminish ought from it" (4:2). The Law given by God at Sinai was not to be edited or amended in any way. Most of us would agree that the Ten Commandments have stood the test of time down through the ages, as a basis both for holistic living and for viable community.

Remember (Chapter 4)
A Call to Obedience

The central theme of this part of Moses' address can be summarized with one word: *Remember!* In fact, the call to remember is one of the central themes of the Bible. The memory of God's faithfulness, and the memory of the drama of the giving of the Covenant at Mount Sinai made the basis for helping us through our daily struggles. Memory that connects us with our past also sustains us in the present. Remembering, though, is much more than merely recalling the past. Rather, it is bringing the meaningful events of our past into the present in such a way that the memory brings hope, courage, and renewal.

In his *Letters and Papers from Prison*, Dietrich Bonhoeffer bore eloquent witness to the power of mem-

The Power of Memory

149

ory. He recalled how the memory of Scripture sustained him in his imprisonment by the Nazis during the second World War. Again and again the memory of a friend or loved one brought strength in time of need. And above all, the memory of God's faithfulness to prophets, saints, and martyrs across the centuries brought hope and renewal. Presbyterian missionary Ben Weir found the memories of Scripture and the awareness of praying friends an inexhaustible source of strength in his imprisonment as a hostage in Lebanon.

We Become What We Remember

Someone has said that we become our memories, for in the deepest sense we tend to live out that which we remember. In remembering, we can recapture and re-create the visions which have shaped our past. It is when we no longer remember who God is and who we are that we become disoriented. Disconnected from our past, it is impossible to connect meaningfully with the present.

A Jealous God?

We cannot leave this part of our Scripture lesson without commenting on verse 24 of Chapter 4, "For the Lord thy God is a consuming fire, even a jealous God." The language may seem harsh to us, but it is always tied to the love of God. In Hebrew, the word translated "jealous" does not mean the kind of envy and anger that we associate with it. It means rather that God stands alone as God; He has no rivals. This idea is expressed clearly in Moses' words, "Know therefore this day, and consider it in thine heart, that the Lord he is God in heaven above and upon the earth beneath: *there is none else* (4:39, italics mine).

A Second Introduction

The section containing Moses' second address begins with verse 1 of Chapter 5 and runs through Chapter 28. However, verses 44 through 49 of Chapter 4 actually give us a second introduction to the Book of Deuteronomy, once again setting the stage.

The Ten Commandments and the Meeting with God (Chapter 5)

In the next seven chapters of the Book of Deuteronomy (5–11) Moses gives his listeners (and readers of all time) a series of appeals to obedience and faithfulness in following God's Law for His people. In this way Moses' listeners are prepared for the explanation of the Law found in Chapters 12 through 26. He also emphasizes here that the Covenant God made with His people at Mount Sinai wasn't just with the previous generation who had died in the wilderness but was for all the people of Israel in any time. The laws were to be learned, kept, and acted upon (5:1-5).

The Need for Standards

As twentieth-century Christians we find ourselves living at a time of great confusion and ambiguity about moral and ethical standards. In a poignant scene in Marc Connelly's play, *Green Pastures,* the Angel Gabriel leans over the parapet of heaven, looking down on earth, and exclaims, "Everything nailed down is comin' loose!"

That's the way it seems in our part of the world. There appears to be a great uncertainty as to absolutes in morals and ethical behavior. Relativism seems to have become a way of life. But thinking people are beginning to see the need for standards. The permissiveness of the past generation or two isn't working.

I believe deeply that a rediscovery of the Ten Commandments, not as rigid rules to be enforced but as principles for life and relationships, could form the basis for a sweeping renewal of integrity and excellence in both our national and international life. Perhaps we need to see these commandments not as an optional list of suggestions for a happy and productive life but as a matter of life or death. National and international survival in a nuclear and space age may indeed demand urgent attention to these commandments.

The First Commandment

This first commandment (5:7) calls for the exclusive worship of "the Lord thy God, which brought thee out of the land of Egypt." Now, it is important for us to realize that the question of "other gods" was by no means the problem only of our ancient spiritual ancestors. It is still *our* greatest problem. In a recent book Richard Foster identifies three false gods of our time—*money, power,* and *sex.*

151

A man in my town—a husband, father, and church member—was recently sentenced to a long prison term for defrauding a number of investors—*money*. The late 1980s has witnessed the breakdown of moral standards on the part of more than one front-page personality—*power* and *sex*. To worship at the modern altars of money, power, and sex delivers brokenness and alienation.

The Second Commandment

The second commandment establishes the ultimate authority of God alone (5:8–10). To bow before any other authority—"any graven image, or any likeness of any thing"—is idolatry and is forbidden.

It is true, of course, in much of the twentieth-century world that idolatry doesn't consist of making golden bull calves or any other object of wood or clay to represent or manipulate God's actions. Rather, for us, idolatry means using anything—worship, material, or intellectual things—in an effort to control or manipulate Him.

The Third Commandment

"Thou shalt not take the name of the Lord thy God in vain" (5:11) signals not only the prohibition of profanity but includes using God's name casually or unworthily. It involves the use of God's name to further our own interests and causes. To honor God's name means that we take Him seriously and deliberately into the day-to-day routines of our lives.

The Fourth Commandment

Here we have a reminder that God is really concerned about our total well-being (5:12–15). The Sabbath Day is a day of worship, rest, and celebration. The emphasis on this rehearsal of the fourth commandment is that God rested after the creation and we, too, are to protect our times of rest and rejuvenation. Our tendency today is to become so distracted by the events of life that we do not celebrate the life God has given us, and we neglect both the worship of God and the learning about Him which are so important to spiritual development.

The Fifth Commandment

The first four commandments have to do with our relationship to God. Now the focus shifts to our relationships with one another. Of primary importance in both ancient and modern society is the honoring of parents (5:16). Since the Covenant was made with adults, I've always assumed the basic meaning of this commandment has to do with the honor and care of our aging parents. I believe this is a vital word for us in modern society as our parents are now living much longer than in past generations.

"Thou shalt not kill" (5:17). Other translations say, in effect, "Thou shalt not commit murder." God places a high value on human life. To commit murder is the ultimate violation of that value.

The Sixth Commandment

The seventh commandment holds marriage and sexual fidelity to be of great importance. The marriage relationship is sacred. Any violation of it is prohibited (5:18).

The Seventh Commandment

This commandment adds the sanctity of property to that of family and marriage (5:19). More is involved in this commandment than burglary or robbery. Later in the Book of Deuteronomy (24:7) we see that a basic intent of this commandment had to do with "manstealing" in which people were stolen and sold for personal profit. We have also come to see that stealing includes robbing another person of his or her good name and attempting to manipulate others for our own profit.

The Eighth Commandment

The thrust of this commandment had to do primarily with the process of law in the courts (5:20). The Hebrew society—the Covenant community— could function only when integrity in the courts was assured. The underlying idea here is that even as God is faithful to us we are to be faithful to each other.

The Ninth Commandment

The tenth commandment differs from the earlier ones because it deals with motives rather than actions (5:21). It is possible this one is the thread that ties the others together, because it speaks to the reasons in the heart that lead to our actions.

In the Sermon on the Mount (Matt. 5–7) Jesus

The Tenth Commandment

placed great emphasis on desires as well as actions. Desire often leads to action, and even when it doesn't, it is still a betrayal of our relationship with God and other people.

The People's Request, the Lord's Answer, and Moses' Challenge

Chapter 5 concludes with a rehearsal of the request the people made of Moses at Horeb (Mount Sinai) to be their mediator with God (5:22–27), the response of the Lord to Moses (5:28–31), and the challenge of Moses to the children of Israel to "walk in all the ways which the Lord your God hath commanded you" (5:32–33).

I just have to believe that the repetition here of the Ten Commandments given originally by God to Moses on Mount Sinai served to impress upon the people the importance of the Law, as well as to teach the Law to a new generation. A rediscovery of this sacred truth, I also believe, is vital to the spiritual development and growth of Christians and to the restoration of sanity, wholeness, justice, and peace to a world that seems to have lost its bearings.

The Greatest Commandment (Chapter 6)

For me, Deuteronomy 6 is one of the greatest chapters in all of the Bible. Certainly, Jesus had a special love for it, for He quoted verse 5 as a summary of the Law and the Prophets (Mark 12:29–31). Verses 4–9, the *Shema,* have been used as the opening sentences in Hebrew worship for centuries, and are repeated by the devout twice daily in conjunction with Deuteronomy 11:13–21 and Numbers 15:37–41. The *Shema* contains the essence of biblical faith and life.

In this chapter the importance of remembering is again stressed. Whether or not the words about binding the commandments upon their hands, hanging them before their eyes, and writing them upon the doorposts of their houses were intended to be taken literally is not clear. But from these words, traditions developed among Jews that continue to this day.

Anyone visiting Israel today can see Jewish men with phylacteries on their forearms and foreheads. These are the little cases containing small scrolls on which are written the words of Deuteronomy 6:4–9 and 11:13–21. Observant Jews also attach a small cylinder (called a *mezuzah*) containing the same passages on the upper part of the right-hand doorpost of their houses.

These literal applications of Moses' words serve as a continuing reminder to Jews of who God is, who they are, and what they are called to be and do. I'm convinced we Christians would be much better off if we too had developed some equivalent of phylacteries and *mezuzot*. How easy it is to move through the

A view of the mountains of Moab as seen from Qumran. It was in a setting not unlike this that was in sight of Israel's camp. Moab was also the setting of the Balak and Balaam story.

hectic schedule of a typical day with very little thought of God. We could use constant reminders that we are to love God with all of our heart, soul, and might.

Three Dangers

Having given them the *Shema,* Moses warned them of three dangers to be avoided after they had entered the Promised Land. The first danger was that material abundance had the potential to dull the keen edge of their relationship with God (6:10–12). The second was the danger of becoming absorbed into the culture and religion of the people around them (6:13–15). The third was the danger of unbelief (6:16), for at Massah (Exod. 17:1–7) they had questioned whether or not God was really with them.

Do not those same dangers exist for us today? Our greed and materialism, our absorption of cultural religion, and our questioning of God are all too prevalent.

Only by remembering, reciting, rehearsing, teaching, and conversing can we hope to remember at all times who God is, who we are, and what we are to be and do (6:17–25).

Called to be Different (Chapter 7)
The Opposition

As Moses moves further into his address, he points out the opposition the children of Israel will confront when they invade Canaan. In verse 1 he lists the seven Canaanite nations they will oppose, all of them larger and mightier than they are. Each of these nations was independent and powerful in its own right. Together in a kind of loose federation they controlled Canaan from the Negev on the south to Syria on the north.

As we read Moses' instructions here (7:1–5), we will likely feel more than a little uneasy over the destruction that is demanded. The scene portrayed in these verses runs counter to our twentieth-century sensitivities. But these are events that are better left to God. The point being made here, though, is terribly important. The inhabitants of the Promised Land were an evil and pagan people. There would be a deadly danger in any kind of commingling, because, as Moses told the Israelites, they were "an holy people unto the Lord thy God: the Lord thy God hath chosen thee to be a special people unto himself, above all people that are upon the face of the earth" (7:6).

As a people chosen and loved by God, they could expect His blessing as long as they kept His commandments (7:7–15). Furthermore, Moses assured them, God would lead them to victory as long as they remained faithful to their calling and exhibited courage based on God's faithfulness rather than their own cleverness and ability (7:16–26).

A People Loved by God

There is one particular member of our church whom I especially enjoy visiting because she has developed the remarkable gift of discovering good in past failures and disappointments. In sharing her experiences, she has so often told about pain and suffering only to follow that up with the lessons she has learned that give her strength and courage. I never leave her presence without being a better person. It's a paradox, I suppose, but so often our growth as persons comes in our hard times.

The Peril of Self-sufficiency (Chapter 8) *Growing Through Adversity*

That seems to be the message that Moses has for his people now. Yes, the forty years of living in the wilderness had been a nightmare from the human perspective. It had been hard, but the Lord had been with them and had led them (8:2). That was the good news; God had been with them even in their adversity. Along with the many lessons they had learned, God had spoken to them through even their hunger. While God had furnished them daily manna which had become a terribly monotonous diet, they had learned that "man doth not live by bread only, but by every word that proceedeth out of the mouth of the Lord" (8:3). You will remember that these are the very words Jesus quoted to His tempter in His wilderness experience.

As Moses continues, he warns his people against misreading God's goodness in giving them the Land of Promise. In spite of the material blessings that would come as they occupied Canaan, they were not

A False Sense of Self-security

157

to settle back in comfort and self-security (8:10–17). Instead, they were to "remember the Lord," otherwise they would be separated from Him (8:18–20).

The Peril of Self-righteousness (9:1–10:11)

Self-righteousness is the destructive handmaiden of self-sufficiency. As Moses continues, he makes this point clear. Promising the Hebrews that they will be victorious over the powerful people and cities of Canaan, he reminds them it will be God's doing and not theirs (9:1–15). He also reminds them of their stubborn and rebellious sinfulness first at Mount Sinai, and then again at Kadesh-barnea (9:6–10:11).

The Wonder of God's Grace

As we read this retelling of their shortcomings and rebellious attitudes and reactions, we can't help but marvel at God's grace. In spite of everything that had happened, they had the assurance that God was with them and that they would "possess the land."

Frequently I've heard the Old Testament characterized as teaching a gospel of works, in contrast to the New Testament, which teaches a gospel of grace. But salvation is as much by grace in the Old Testament as it is in the New, and this point is clearly made in our Scripture lesson. The New Testament counterpart to these words from Deuteronomy is found in Paul's letter to the church at Ephesus, "For by grace are ye saved through faith; and that not of yourselves: it is the gift of God: Not of works, lest any man should boast" (Eph. 2:8–9).

What Does the Lord Require? (10:12–11:32)

This part of Moses' address now moves to a compassionate appeal for responsive action in obedience and love. In a few choice words spelled out for his listeners, Moses tells what God expects of them. These words are as true for us today as they were for the children of Israel over three thousand years ago, "And now, Israel, what doth the Lord thy God require of thee, but *to fear the Lord thy God, to walk in all his ways, and to love him, and to serve the Lord thy God with all thy heart and with all thy soul*" (10:12–13, italics mine).

That's it! To fear God is to honor Him with reverence and worship. It is to worship Him with awe and wonder. It is to love and obey Him. The reference to circumcising the "foreskin of your heart" is a figure of speech calling for openness to God's word and will (10:16). Uncircumcision was a sign of disobedience.

As you read the rest of the verses in the Scripture lesson, they may seem redundant and repetitious. But we must remember that the Hebrews were an oral people. Moses was delivering an oral address, and repetition was common to that tradition.

The Reward for Obedience

Toward the end of this part of Moses' speech, he assures the children of Israel that they will be blessed if they obey the Lord's commandments. At the same time he warns them that if they disobey the Lord and turn to other gods, they will receive a curse (11:26–28).

Love and obedience to the will of God are our birthright. God has been faithful to all He has promised throughout human history. He went so far as to give His own Son for our salvation; He is worthy of our trust, love, and obedience!

Lord God, Help me to revere You, to walk in all Your ways, to love You, and to serve You with all my heart and soul. Let this kind of complete devotion to You characterize my days. AMEN.

WHAT THIS SCRIPTURE MEANS TO ME
Deuteronomy 1–11

I am a World War 2 buff and I've seen many movies about that memorable period. One of the first movies I saw was a film on D-Day, the Allied invasion of Normandy in France. I remember scenes of the troops practicing their maneuvers—shooting, parachuting, unloading from boats—practicing until the men were ready for action.

The night before the troops were supposed to cross the English channel, everybody gathered for the final briefing. The men listened earnestly to the voice of their leader. Their faces were tense, their bodies taut. Two things were important: understanding the final instructions, and remembering to apply their training correctly. Carelessness or distractions or slipping out of practice could mean death in the months ahead.

Our lesson reminds me in some ways of that film. On the eve of the invasion of Canaan, Moses gave the Israelites their final briefing. They had been living under the Law for almost forty years, learning how to be God's people. They knew that following God's Law was directly related to their success in battle.

In his farewell speech, Moses emphasized the special relationship Israel had as God's chosen nation. Moses repeatedly reminded them not to worship the gods of the people they would conquer. God, he warned, was a jealous God, and idolatry would be disastrous both spiritually and politically.

As the Israelites listened to Moses, I'm sure they were anxious to claim the Promised Land. Like the troops before D-Day, they were in many ways ready for the battle. Also, they knew that the final instructions were extremely important. Moses didn't want the people to slip into worshiping other gods. Continued obedience to God and to the Law could mean the difference between the life and death of the nation.

On a personal level, this lesson reminds me of a CPR class I took several years ago. For three hours one evening, a group of us listened to the instructor explain how to revive a person who has stopped breathing. He demonstrated artificial resuscitation on the dummy "Resusca Annie."

Then each of us practiced putting the CPR principles into use. We practiced until we passed the test.

The next few weeks I reviewed the CPR method in my mind, constantly on the lookout for heart attack victims whose lives might be saved by my timely expertise. As the months went by, though, I became involved in other activities, and I slowly began to forget how to do CPR.

Today, if I witnessed someone having a heart attack, all I could do is run for the telephone. In a potential matter of life and death, I have let my training slip.

As we have seen in past lessons, the Israelites often let their faith in God slip. Moses' farewell speech is a powerful retraining session in the importance of loving God and keeping His commandments.

In my own life, I need to be reminded often—in sermons, in the Bible, in books, in worship services—to love God and live my life as a Christian. It is easy to let self-interest and other distractions slide in and take over. Before I know it, my relationship with God has slipped.

Like the Israelites, we have a choice as to what comes first in our lives, not only when we face something as important as a battle, but in the day-to-day routines as well. Moses' reminder can be our own: "And thou shalt love the Lord thy God with all thine heart, and with all thy soul, and with all thy might" (Deut. 6:5).

It is still a matter of life and death.

LESSON 7
Deuteronomy 12–26

Living the Ten Commandments

Dear Lord, May Your Word be a light to my feet and a lamp to my path. May the ancient Word be Your Word to me. AMEN.

The fifteen chapters in our Scripture lesson are called the Deuteronomic Code, a section in which the Ten Commandments are expanded and applied. In reading these chapters, you will find it tempting to skip over most of the material as having little relevance for us today. Being told not to eat camel's meat or falcon or ostrich probably won't make a significant difference in your life. And being told to cancel all debts at the end of every seven years isn't likely to fly with your friendly banker.

We will read more than seventy laws in this part of Moses' second address, as he tries to prepare the people of Israel for their entry into the Promised Land after forty years in the wilderness. Among these "statutes and ordinances" are appeals by Moses for the people to live faithful and obedient lives.

Two Extremes

I believe we must avoid either of two dangerous extremes in studying this part of Deuteronomy. The

162

first is to relegate most of it to the realm of interesting facts pertaining only to our understanding of antiquity. To do this is to find little that applies directly to us.

The second danger is in trying to apply all of these laws literally as though they were meant for all places and times. If we succumb to this extreme, we discover that eating pork is forbidden forever, and a "stubborn and rebellious" son who has refused the correction of his parents is to be stoned to death by all the men of his city.

I find two principles to be helpful in reading this part of Deuteronomy. The first is that the "statutes and ordinances" of Deuteronomy 12–26 were not intended to be timeless laws or codes. Only the Covenant given at Mount Sinai was timeless.

Two Principles for Understanding

What we have in Chapters 12 through 26 is the way in which Moses and the people of Israel applied the principles of the Ten Commandments to specific areas of their lives. It was *their* understanding of how they were to apply the Covenant more than three thousand years ago—as they began life in a foreign land among people with religious beliefs and practices repugnant to theirs. Obviously, there will be much about their beliefs and traditions that will seem both strange and unacceptable to us.

The second helpful principle for me is the realization that these "statutes and ordinances" can still have significance for us if we search for their deeper meanings. It is true, of course, because of the lapse of time, our search will not always lead us to a clear understanding, but I believe our reflections on the Deuteronomic Code as we have it here will bring us to a fuller understanding of the application of the Ten Commandments in our own lives.

The verdict of a nineteenth-century Old Testament scholar is a reminder to us of the unique value of the Book of Deuteronomy, "Nowhere else in the Old Testament do we breathe such an atmosphere of generous devotion to God, and of large-hearted benevolence towards man; nowhere else are duties and

The Unique Value of Deuteronomy

motives set forth with greater depth or tenderness of feeling, or with more winning and persuasive eloquence; and nowhere else is it shown with the same fulness of detail how high and noble principles may be applied so as to elevate and refine the entire life of the community."

Our approach to the Deuteronomic Code will be to divide it into five sections, for the most part following the Scripture text itself:

12:1–16:17—The Purity of Worship
16:18–18:22—The Qualities of Leadership
19 & 21:1–9—Criminal Law
20 & 21:10–25:16—Miscellaneous Laws about
Civil and Domestic Matters
26—The Concluding Exhortation

The Purity of Worship (12:1–16:17)

This first section of what we know as the Deuteronomic Code is devoted to provisions that regulate the purity and integrity of worship, and represents about one-third of the entire code. The amount of space given to this part of their life indicates just how important worship was to the people of Israel. For them, regular devotion in worship was a constant reminder of God's sovereignty and continuing presence with them.

No Tolerance of Pagan Deities

If the worship of the children of Israel was to be pure and acceptable to God, there could be no toleration of the Canaanite gods when the Hebrews moved into the Land of Promise. Loyalty to and worship of a variety of gods and goddesses was the accepted pattern of the pagan culture of the ancient world, but the Israelites' devotion must be to one God.

So, Moses now tells the people that when they occupy Canaan, they are to "utterly destroy" all the Canaanite places of worship (12:2). This included overthrowing their altars and breaking their pillars—upright stone objects present near the altars in all Canaanite places of worship. In addition, they were to "burn their groves [Asherim] with fire," symbols of the goddess Asherah. In other words, they were to utterly wipe out every semblance and symbol of pagan worship (12:3). Moses wanted to make sure nothing was left to contaminate their worship of the one true and living God.

This attention to detail may seem like overplaying things a bit. But if Israel's worship was to remain pure, there could be no divided loyalties. This truth is just as vital for us in our Christian pilgrimage today as it was for our spiritual ancestors camped on the east side of the Jordan River over three thousand years ago. Our gods aren't known as Baal or Ashtoreth but as money, power, family, job, social sta-

It was Canaanite altars like the one pictured here that the children of Israel were to utterly destroy. Note the "horns."

tus, sex—anyone or anything that moves God out of the number one role in life.

A Central Place and Forms of Worship

Major emphasis is given next to the establishment of a central place of worship—a central sanctuary, a place where the Ark of the Covenant would be permanently located (12:4–14). All during the wilderness wanderings of the children of Israel the Tabernacle—the place where God dwelt—was positioned in the middle of the camp. Later, as we shall see, the Tabernacle was moved from place to place during the conquest of Canaan until it was finally located at Shiloh. There it remained during the period of the judges. And, of course, the idea of a central place for worship found its ultimate fulfillment in the building of the Temple in Jerusalem by Solomon.

The Hebrew pattern of a central place of worship, the place where God is, stood in sharp contrast to the many local Canaanite shrines. The Hebrews were to worship in the place chosen by their God—the place where He would "put his name" (12:5).

Also in this part of our Scripture lesson Moses looks ahead and speaks of certain modifications in their sacrificial worship forms. For example, according to the original giving of the Law the only source of meat for the Hebrews came from the animal sacrifices made at the Tabernacle. This was all right as long as the children of Israel were all clustered around the Tabernacle. But with the settling of Canaan where the majority of people would be away from their central sanctuary, an alternative plan was needed. So now a distinction is made between animals killed for sacrifice and those killed as a source of food (12:15–22).

With this provision the Hebrews could now kill animals at home for food with the only restriction being that there should not be blood in the meat (12:16, 23). As we learned in our Leviticus studies, blood was regarded as the source of life, and as such, it belonged only to God.

The Focus of Our Worship Is a Person

These particular Old Testament worship rules have little direct application for us. The center of our worship is no longer in a place but in a Person. As the pastor of one congregation among many in a community, I sometimes am tempted to wish for a unifying center in which all Christians might gather for worship. Such an approach, however, would lead to a system that would most likely become too rigid and stilted.

The Deuteronomic concept of a single and central place of worship was obviously important for the people of Israel at that time in history. But for us, Jesus Christ is present wherever "two or three" are gathered in His name (Matt. 18:20). The purity of our worship is determined by our closeness to Christ and not by a particular location.

As Moses continues, purity of worship is still the issue. He warns against the temptation to mix worship of the one true God with worship of the Canaanite gods (12:29–13:18). In the light of the first two of the Ten Commandments we see that nothing could be more heinous than the sin of idolatry.

The Temptation to Idolatry

Three possible sources of enticement into idolatry are anticipated in our Scripture lesson: false prophets (13:1–5); family members or close friends (13:6–11); and an entire community of people (13:12–18).

The people of Israel had high regard for prophets. And there was the natural tendency to give greater credibility to the words of a prophet if he "giveth thee a sign or a wonder" (13:1). But Moses' words make it clear that miraculous signs don't authenticate the words of a prophet. Rather, it is the integrity of the prophet's message as he speaks the truth of God that counts.

Then comes the warning against being enticed into an idolatrous relationship by any member of the family or by any person within the community. In other words the temptation to worship other gods, irrespective of where and who it comes from, is to be rejected vigorously. In fact, the penalties spelled out in these verses against anyone who attempted to lead a person astray into idolatry seem not only harsh but inconceivable to us.

It is true, of course, that we can't move back more

than three thousand years into the ancient Israelite culture and identify directly with them. But we must remember that idolatry struck at the very roots of their national and spiritual life. As a theocracy, the ultimate form of treason was idolatry. As a community of God, the ultimate betrayal was to lead someone away from loyalty to God.

Yes, all of this seems worlds away from our immediate concerns as we try to raise our families and carve out a niche in our complex society. But the warning sounded by the Deuteronomy writer against idolatry in any of its forms and against tempting others to substitute anyone or anything for God is to be taken seriously. We are to be ruthless with ourselves in making certain that our loyalties are centered in God.

The Importance of Being Different

The "statutes and ordinances" on purity of worship continue in Chapter 14:1–21 with the appeal to avoid some customs and practices probably associated closely with Canaanite religion. Most likely, the practices of self-laceration and shaving the front of one's head were mourning customs in the foreign religions and to be avoided (14:1).

The laws pertaining to clean and unclean foods (14:3–21) are virtually the same as those discussed in Leviticus 11. The central idea here is that the people of Israel were to be different from the people around them.

Some Bible students believe that the dietary restrictions were for sanitary and hygienic reasons. Others argue that the basic issue was that of avoiding eating the meat of animals, fish, birds, and insects that were in some way held sacred by the foreign religions. There seems to be some merit in both ideas. We do know that the prohibition against boiling a kid in its mother's milk (14:21) is a clear protest against the Canaanite practice of preparing a sacrifice by cooking it in milk.

By the time of Jesus, the Jewish laws against clean and unclean foods had been expanded to a complex and cumbersome volume of legislation. Not only did the rules apply to the food itself, but also to the manner of eating. I suggest you stop a moment and read Mark 7:1–23. In this scene Jesus put Himself squarely against the Pharisees and their many rules about ceremonial cleanness and uncleanness. He insisted that ethical and moral purity was much more important than ceremonial cleanness. It is what comes from within that defiles a person.

The Obligation to Tithe

Right in the middle of Moses' lecture on the necessity of purity of worship is the basic statement in all the Bible about the tithe (14:22–29). So often in my role as a pastor I'm confronted by people who want to separate their finances from their worship. I'm painfully aware that many churches, religious organizations, and television ministries have gone to extremes in their demands for money. But greedy and unethical religious fund-raising is no excuse for not recognizing the biblical principle of tithing.

For the people of ancient Israel tithing was required, but beyond that, it was to be a blessing and not a burden to the tither. The tithe was to be a source of celebration for the goodness of God and His abundant provision for them. It was a constant reminder that everything belonged to God and that all good things come from Him.

The Year of "Release"

Hand in hand with the law of the tithe is the provision for the cancellation of debts every seventh year (15:1–11). By human standards this kind of action seems unthinkable, but as these verses reveal, God's standards are drastically different. For the Hebrews, the welfare of every person was of primary importance, and this applied especially to those who were poor and in need (15:7–11).

One of the most misused and abused comments of Jesus, "For the poor always ye have with you" (John 12:8), actually originated in our Deuteronomy lesson, "For the poor shall never cease out of the land" (15:11). Jesus spoke those words because Judas had labeled as wasteful the use of the "precious ointment" by Mary of Bethany when she poured some of it on Jesus' head not long before His death.

Jesus and His hearers knew the source of those

169

words well, and were aware that the reference was to the importance of being generous to the poor because they would always be with us. In fact the rest of verse 11 reads, "Thou shalt open thine hand wide unto thy brother, to thy poor, and to the needy, in thy land." This was a powerful call to the children of Israel to always be generous with the poor, and it is a model for Christian compassion and action today.

Freedom for the Servant-Slave

The law of generosity in the seventh year, the year of release, also applied to releasing the servant-slave who because of poverty had become indentured to a fellow Israelite (15:12–18). In other words, this unfortunate person could not become the *permanent* property of another, but would be released during the seventh year. He could, however, if he wished, stay on in his position. It was also provided that during the period of servitude the "slave" was to be treated well and helped in every reasonable way.

The Consecration of Firstborn Animals

The closing words of Chapter 15 emphasize the law that all the firstborn of their animals that were without blemish of any kind were dedicated to the Lord. This, of course, was a continual reminder of the salvation of their firstborn sons in Egypt. The first and the best was always reserved for God.

We have too readily accepted the idea that our money and our property belong to us to do with as we please. But that is not the teaching of this part of our Deuteronomy lesson or of Jesus. Everything we have belongs to God and is to be used to meet not only our needs but also the needs of the poor and the hungry wherever they are.

Let's Celebrate!

The portion of Moses' address devoted to purity of worship comes to a fitting conclusion in the highlighting of the three principal Jewish feasts: Passover, Pentecost and Tabernacles (16:1–17).

The Feast of Passover (16:1–8), as we learned in our studies in Leviticus and Numbers, was the annual celebration of their deliverance from slavery in Egypt. The central act of Passover was the sacrifice of the paschal lamb—the symbol of the ultimate fulfillment of our freedom from slavery to sin through the death of Jesus, the Lamb of God who takes away the sins of the world (John 1:29).

The Feast of Pentecost (16:9–12) was also called the Feast of Weeks because it was celebrated seven weeks after Passover. It was also known as the Feast of First Fruits because it was the celebration of the completion of the wheat harvest. Pentecost has profound meaning for Christians, for it was on that day following the death and resurrection of Jesus that the Holy Spirit came with power on that first group of believers.

The Feast of Tabernacles or Booths (16:13–15) followed the fall harvest and was a most joyous occasion. Its name came from the little booths of branches each family built and in which they stayed during the celebration, to remind them of the forty years of living in tents.

The Importance of Remembering

The male members of all of the tribes of Israel were to attend these times of celebration in a central place—later in their history it would be in Jerusalem (16:16–17). These were to be times of celebration and generosity and were to include everyone.

The act of *remembering* is important to us as Christians. Celebration of the events of the Christian year—Christmas, Easter, Pentecost—are helpful reminders of all that it means to be believers in Jesus Christ. Unfortunately, some of these times have been commercialized by contemporary society. But as we act to recover the true meaning of these times of celebration, our lives as persons and as a church will be enriched.

The Qualities of Leaders (16:18–18:22)
The Conduct of Judges

Fundamental to every community or social order is the proper administration of justice. Moses' instructions are very clear as to what is involved, "Thou shalt not wrest [pervert] judgment; thou shalt not respect persons [show favoritism], neither take a gift [bribe]. . . . That which is altogether just shalt thou follow, that thou mayest live, and inherit the land which the Lord thy God giveth thee" (16:19–20).

Even today, justice becomes perverted through

171

partiality and bribery, and it can so easily become the means whereby the affluent are privileged above the poor, and racial majorities are favored above minorities. Complete honesty and impartiality are everybody's due.

Moses' next remarks (16:21–17:7) may seem to revert back to the purity in worship section, but here judges and leaders are all reminded that public life and service and worship of God are intended to be inseparable. There is no distinction in the Bible between a private faith and a public faith. After all, private faith is always expressed in a commitment—or lack of it—to justice for everyone, and public faith is grounded in personal devotion to the living God.

Before leaving his discussion of justice, Moses provides for a system of appeal. When needed there would be a higher level of justice in the central sanctuary with priests and a judge serving as an appellate court (17:8–13).

Provisions for a King

The provisions given in our Scripture lesson for a king (17:14–20) have been a matter of speculation, since this is the only time in the Pentateuch, the Hebrew Torah—Genesis, Exodus, Leviticus, Numbers, and Deuteronomy—that the idea of kingship is mentioned. The Hebrews poised on the border of Canaan were living under a theocracy—a God-ruled society. However, it is likely this is in anticipation of the future time when human kings might be needed.

Of primary importance was the recognition that any king must be chosen and appointed by God (17:15). Next follow specific instructions as to a king's behavior with regard to horses, wives, and money (17:16–17).

Even though we may chuckle at this combination, the instructions here are very profound. The reference to horses has to do with military might and power—the way of God's people is not the way of military strength. Israel's kings were not to put their faith in horses and chariots.

The reference to wives has specific application to the custom of ancient times. Wives frequently represented political alliances with foreign powers. For example, when a king of Israel married a Pharaoh's daughter, an alliance was formed between Israel and Egypt. But, it is made clear here that the pattern of life for God's people was not to be one of political maneuvering and manipulation.

Moses concluded this section on wise kingly conduct with the warning, "Neither shall he greatly multiply to himself silver and gold" (17:17). The warning was sound. The insatiable pursuit of personal wealth carries with it a corrupting power.

All of this sounds very up-to-date. And while the provisions here were to apply to the kings of ancient Israel, we still catch a very practical application to our twentieth-century life. Our source of strength and guidance, our ability to make right choices and live rich, full lives, is not found in the size of our bank account or in manipulating people or in acquiring power of any kind. It is in faithful service to a loving Lord who cares deeply about our twenty-four-hour efforts to live for Him.

Priests and Levites were set apart for the Lord's service, and Moses' instructions in the first part of Chapter 18 gave the pattern for their support by the rest of the people (18:1–8). Without this support the "clergy-persons" of ancient Israel could not have performed their duties.

Next follows a warning that was so important it merited repetition. Again and again the warning comes not to take on any of the customs and attitudes of the pagan Canaanites when they occupy the land (18:9–14). Moses worded it this way, "Thou shalt be perfect with the Lord thy God" (18:13)—they were to be enthusiastically wholehearted in their service for the Lord.

Following that warning comes the marvelous promise that God would in the future raise up a succession of prophets like Moses, who would be faithful to the integrity of God's Word (18:15–22). These words have come to be understood not only as assuring the faithful proclamation of God's Word to the people of Israel but also as pointing toward the coming of that One Prophet who would be the true

Priests and Levites and Prophets

successor of Moses, Jesus Christ. After Jesus' ascension, the Apostle Peter in his sermon on Solomon's Porch of the Temple saw Jesus as the fulfillment of this early promise (Acts 3:22–25).

Jesus as Prophet, Priest, and King

It is clear here and elsewhere in our Bible story that the three leadership types in ancient Israel were prophets, priest, and kings. As Christians, we see Jesus as the supreme embodiment of all three. He is the Prophet who speaks the truth of God to us in words and actions. He is the Priest who gave Himself as the complete sacrifice for sin and who intercedes with God for us. And he is our King of kings and Lord of lords.

Criminal Law (Chapters 19 and 21:1–9)

In Chapter 19 we find the provisions of the Deuteronomic Code for the administration of justice covering three criminal offenses: murder, both intentional and unintentional; stealing of land; and evidence required in the establishing of guilt. I have also linked the paragraph in Chapter 21:1–9 with Chapter 19 as it deals with another type of murder.

Unintentional Homicide

After reminding the people that they were to set up "cities of refuge" in their new homeland (19:1–3), a provision we studied in Numbers 35:9–34, Moses reviews again the purpose of the cities, and gives directions for dealing with unintentional homicide (19:4–10).

As we mentioned earlier, the law of retaliation was very much a part of ancient culture. When a person was killed, his death could be avenged by the nearest male relative, who became "the avenger of the blood" (19:6). However, in the case of an accidental homicide the person guilty of the death could escape to a city of refuge. There, if he actually could prove the act had been unintentional, he was safe from the retaliation of the dead person's avenger.

Intentional Homicide

However, in the case of premeditated or intentional murder, when the murderer attempted to obtain refuge in one of the cities, the elders of that city could turn the guilty person over to the next of kin who was then free to exact the blood revenge (19:11–13).

Cities of Refuge

The cities of refuge were established to protect anyone who had accidently committed a murder from a hasty execution. Their protection allowed time for cooling off during the investigation to determine culpability or innocence.

Actually, the cities of refuge were a statement of mercy. Their existence placed a restraint on the all-too-human tendency to respond to violence with violence when all the facts aren't in. The stain in our own history left by lynch mobs acting in passion bears eloquent witness to the need for protecting the rights of the accused as well as those of the victim. In this part of our Scripture lesson, the provision of justice made possible through these rulings was a big step forward in the administration of justice in these early stages of Israel's history.

Property Rights

Property rights are always a source of conflict and litigation in every society. It was customary in ancient times to mark property lines with stone markers (19:14). The prohibition is stated here against moving a neighbor's marker so as to acquire added footage or acreage. To do so constituted a theft and violated the commandment against stealing.

The Provision for Witnesses and the Giving of Evidence

The fair administration of justice is dependent on honest and reliable testimony. In order to insure fairness, the principle is established here of requiring testimony from two or three witnesses (19:15–21). In the event of perjury, the false witness was given the penalty that would have been inflicted on the one accused.

In fact, the much misunderstood principle of a life for a life, an eye for an eye, a tooth for a tooth, and a foot for a foot was a step of mercy in the ancient world, because it put limits on vengeance in legal settings and better guaranteed justice.

It was this principle that Jesus made reference to in discussing our personal relationships when He said, "Ye have heard that it hath been said, An eye for an eye, and a tooth for a tooth: But I say unto you, That ye resist not evil [an evil person]: but whosoever shall smite thee on thy right cheek, turn to him the other also. . . . Give to him that asketh thee, and from him that would borrow of thee turn not thou away" (Matt. 5:38–42).

An Unsolved Murder

In the event that a person was killed but the murderer was not known, the entire community was to accept responsibility (21:1–9). Careful instructions are given here as to the sacrificial procedures to be taken by the community leaders to right the wrong that has been done. All sin must be cleansed under the Law.

Civil and Domestic Procedures (Chapters 20 and 21:10–25:16)

Beginning with Chapter 20 and its code for the Holy War, the material through Chapter 25 consists of a collection of miscellaneous laws covering a wide range of relationships and giving us some glimpses into various, and sometimes (to us) strange, customs and practices of ancient Israel. We shall not study in detail all of the laws in this miscellaneous collection, but shall view them under some general headings.

Laws Concerning War

Israel believed in war that was waged on behalf of God and in which God was regarded as an active participant. Though they might be faced with overwhelming odds, they were not to fear, "For the Lord your God is he that goeth with you, to fight for you against your enemies, to save you" (20:4).

This kind of war grew out of zeal to honor God's name and to be faithful to the Covenant. We need not see the Israelites as bloodthirsty monsters intent solely on the destruction of their enemies. Rather, they were committed to the elimination of polytheistic religions and false gods. To them, everything other than the true and pure worship of God must be eliminated (20:1–20).

The instructions for waging war in the conquest of Canaan seem extremely harsh to those of us studying these lessons. But when seen in light of the grim and cruel realities of the surrounding cultures, they are more understandable. In addition, the wars in our century in Europe and Asia have left ugly stains on our own history. Even as I write, readers of today's news are beseiged with holy war horror stories coming out of the Middle East and Northern Ireland. Fighting for the honor of God and country has a long and troubled history.

But the perspective of Jesus calls for a new understanding of the way we conduct our relationships. He lifted up a higher and more perfect way when He said, "Love your enemies, do good to them which hate you, Bless them that curse you, and pray for them which despitefully use you" (Luke 6:27–28). Sound impractical? Yes, by our human standards. But the rules for Christ's new society—the fellowship of Christian believers—cannot be measured by human standards.

An Amalgam of Regulations

It would be easy to become confused while reading the list of regulations and comments on them found between Chapter 21:10 and the end of Chapter 25. There is no particular continuity or progression. Yet, to the people of ancient Israel, our spiritual ancestors, each and every one of these regulations was full of practical meaning. While many of them have no direct application to us today, the spiritual values and directives of some of them are as valid today as when they were first given.

Marriage and Family

The concern expressed throughout the entire Book of Deuteronomy for healthy marriage and family relationships is especially appropriate for our time. While the instructions given in Chapter 21:15–17 concerned primarily the children of a polygamous marriage, a custom allowed in the ancient Near East, the principle of fairness and parental impartiality is as important now as then.

Sexual morality and the sacredness of marriage is addressed in Chapter 22:13–30. And while religious prostitution was prevalent in ancient Near Eastern religions, the people of Israel were forbidden the exercise of this pagan and immoral practice (23:17–18).

Relationships with Relatives and Neighbors

Certain of the regulations in this section governing relationships with relatives and neighbors carry

177

meaning for us as well. The instruction to help a neighbor in need—not just when it is convenient but when a need exists—is found in Chapter 22:1–4. The writer of our New Testament Book of James (2:14–17) understood the spirit of Moses' words when he wrote, "What doth it profit, my brethren, though a man say he hath faith, and have not works? can faith save him?" The answer follows: if a brother or sister is in need, they are to have our help, otherwise our Christian witness lacks meaning.

In Chapter 23:19–20 a statement of relationship is found concerning the lending of money and the charging of interest. Again, the message here is care for our brother and fairness in business dealings. In Chapter 25:13–16 instructions are given governing honesty and fairness in business dealings. The issue here is honest weights and measures, but the spirit of these instructions, along with Jesus' teachings, extends to every part of our business and social relationships.

Cleanliness

In Chapter 23:9–14 we find important instructions concerning hygiene in Israel's camp. Cleanliness, personal and public hygiene, were, and are, matters of concern to God—then and now. This is something in our modern society most of us take for granted. But there are those parts of even our twentieth-century world that are not blessed as we are, where people are living in misery and filth and are dying of diseases caused by unsanitary conditions. Because God cares, we dare not look the other way. Those people are our brothers and sisters, too.

A Holy People

Throughout this part of our lesson and the Book of Deuteronomy as a whole we see that the controlling conviction of the people of Israel was that they were chosen by God to be His people—a holy people. Any practice and any action that corrupted their relationship with God and each other must be avoided at all cost. They were not to compromise that relationship by uncleanness of any kind.

Jesus made it clear that while we are *in* the world, we are not *of* the world. Yes, we are to be responsible

members of society, but as people of God, our lives—
our customs, habits, attitudes, and relationships—are
to be lived according to His plan as made possible
through Jesus Christ.

The Conclusion of Moses' Second Message

In these final words of Moses' second message
(Chapter 26), provision is made for two regular rituals of giving and a final call for obedience.

The first was the provision for bringing a basket of
the firstfruits of the harvest to the central place of
worship, probably at the time of the Feast of Weeks
(16:1–11). This offering became a symbol of gratitude
to God for His continuing and faithful love.

The second ritual of giving described here was to
take place every three years (16:12–15). At this time
a tithe of their increase was to be brought to the place
of worship for distribution to "the Levite, the stranger [aliens], the fatherless [orphans], and the widow,
that they may eat within thy gates, and be filled"
(16:12).

Finally, Moses reminds the people that obedience
to the Holiness Code is essential to their worship—
and their relationship with the Lord as "an holy people unto the Lord thy God" (26:19). The phrase, "The
Lord thy God," appears 299 times in the Book of
Deuteronomy and stresses their special relationship
with the one and only Creator-God. They were to
understand in all of this that obedience to God called
for them to live in loving and caring relationships
with each other.

*Father God, You alone are the Lord. You are my God. You are
my Master. You are the Lord my God. AMEN.*

LESSON 7

179

WHAT THIS SCRIPTURE MEANS TO ME
Deuteronomy 12—26

One summer my family went to Colorado for a vacation. We stayed for a week at a family camp high in the cool, beautiful Rockies. My sister and I made friends with some of the other children, and by the middle of the week, we had decided to form a children's club.

I remember sitting around a table in the dining room planning excitedly. We outlined our club's purpose, gave ourselves a name, and even instituted an initiation rite: Anyone willing to drink our special concoction of water and condiments could be a member of our club.

On an adult level, I had two great-aunts who were charter members of a campus organization at Oklahoma University. By the time I went to OU, the organization was well established. But I can imagine my aunts' excitement at being on the ground floor of the new group as they met with the national leader to define goals and write the by-laws. It must have been very important to establish all the ways the organization touched the lives of the members—in social and charitable activities, in grades, in friendships, and in other common aspects in the life of the group.

In our lesson, the Israelites were, in a sense, charter members of a new religion. As their leader, Moses knew how important it was that the people have a firm understanding of their purpose and the rules. In his review of the laws God gave them, Moses interprets and explains how the laws affect the Israelites' daily life.

As I read over this section of Deuteronomy, I was struck with the scope of the commandments. God cared about every detail of the peoples' lives. He wasn't just concerned with how they worshiped Him; He was interested in their social, political, and family life as well.

For example, God cared about the way the Israelites handled money, especially their debts. In addition, He wanted the people to care for the poor, to treat slaves well, to use proper sanitation. God showed His interest in their marriages, in their crops, in the spoils of war, and in inheritance affairs. He was concerned with details such as the kind of seed planted in their vineyards, the weights and measures used in business transactions, and their property boundaries. At all times, God was present in the very center of the Israelites' activities, weaving His love and care throughout the texture of their daily lives.

What this says to me today is that God is still interested in every part of our lives. He still cares about details. Sometimes it is easy to put God into a compartment labeled "Religious activities," and then exclude Him from the more mundane parts of our existence, like going to work or school, or cleaning the house.

One time last year I was planning a party. I had already bought the invitations, but I was having a hard time deciding who should be on my guest list. Finally, I asked God to help me decide who to invite. At first I felt apologetic for bothering Him with something so seemingly small, but then I realized perhaps it wasn't so small after all. After reading our lesson, I'm convinced of it.

God wants to be integrated into the fabric of our lives. As He showed the Israelites, He cares for us so much that He is willing to become involved even in the things we think are trivial.

LESSON 8
Deuteronomy 27–34

Renewal and Commitment

Dear Lord: As men and women of old renewed their commitment to You, may I renew mine in the Spirit of Your love. Amen.

Some Bible students see Moses' third major address or message as beginning with Chapter 27 and concluding with Chapter 30. However, it is my feeling that only Chapters 29 and 30 actually make up Moses' third major message to his people.

I also hold the position that Chapters 27 and 28 are best understood when studied in reverse order. In other words Chapter 28 seems more logically to follow after Chapter 26. And then Chapter 27, which anticipates the Covenant renewal ceremony on Mount Ebal and Mount Gerizim, would logically follow the content of Chapter 28.

Chapters 31 through 34 bring the story of Moses to a close. We're told here how Joshua, the new leader, was chosen, and how Moses passed from the scene. We will shape our study in Lesson 8 around these three sections and in the order outlined above.

As I've already mentioned, first read Chapter 28 as a continuation of Chapter 26. Chapter 28 opens with Moses promising the people that they will be blessed if they obey God. At the same time he warns them that they will be cursed if they disobey Him.

The structure of Chapter 28 is fascinating. Read verses 3–6 alongside of verses 16–19. The two sections are practically identical, except for the initial word of each clause, indicating that there will be either a blessing or a curse in every aspect and condition of their lives. Verses 7–14 expand upon the promise of blessing, giving specific examples of ways in which the blessings will be experienced. Verses 20–68 are a much more lengthy expansion of the types of curses that will follow upon their disobedience. The warnings outnumber the promises eight-to-one.

When we read Chapter 27, we see how some of these curses were to be used in a dramatic ceremony of renewal after they crossed the Jordan River into Canaan and moved into the hill country just south of Shechem, near the site of Abraham's well (27:2–13). The actual ceremony is described in Joshua 8:30–35.

Carrying stones whitewashed with lime, they were to build an altar upon Mount Ebal. On the stones, they were to write very plainly "all the words of this law" (27:8). They were then to celebrate the occasion with burnt offerings and peace offerings. You will recall from our lessons in Leviticus that in the peace offerings, the worshipers ate some of the food that had been offered. The picture here is one of celebration, like a modern-day picnic—a joyous party.

Then there follows something of an antiphonal litany between the six tribes standing on Mount Gerizim and the other six directly across the valley, on Mount Ebal. On Gerizim was a litany of blessing, not included in our text, and on Ebal was a litany of curses, with the Levites chanting the curse and the people responding with "Amen!" Imagine what it

The Blessings and the Curses (Chapters 27 and 28)

The Scene on Mount Ebal and Mount Gerizim

Blessings As a Response to Obedience? Curses As a Response to Disobedience?

would have been like if you could have stood between the two mountains listening to this service!

Without elaborating on the many blessings and the many more curses in these two chapters, we note in reading them that they consisted of national and individual sins. It is obvious that this service of renewal there in the valley near Shechem between the two mountains would penetrate the hearts and minds of the people dramatically. What a reminder this was to be that God had glorious plans for them as a nation, as they occupied land He had promised them! At the same time this service was a solemn reminder that their selection by God to be His special people would not automatically convey His blessings upon them. Their obedience to the Covenant was a condition for God's blessing.

This theme of blessing for obedience and curses for disobedience is very much a part of Israel's history. Obedience to the Law would bring Israel national and individual prosperity, health, security, and power in international relationships. Disobedience to the Law would bring God's judgment.

Difficult Questions

As we reflect on this pattern for the people of Israel over three thousand years ago, we confront two questions. One, on a day-to-day basis, can we as people and as a nation be sure that obedience produces observable blessing and disobedience produces God's immediate and observable punishment? Two, is human suffering always a sign of God's punishment for disobedience? To both of these questions I have to answer with an emphatic *No!*

I share a close relationship with one of my staff pastors, a man in his mid-thirties. Three years ago he was diagnosed as having Parkinson's disease, which causes a lack of coordination and control in the central nervous system resulting in tremors and loss of muscle control, especially in the arms and legs. As I've watched my friend's disease progress, and knowing him as I do, any question of his illness as a punishment from God is ludicrous.

On the other hand, I know another man who is

extremely sharp in business and who has the reputation in the marketplace of being a ruthless driver of hard bargains, a martinet who gives no quarter, and who is quick to sacrifice people for profit. This man is generally respected in the community, is well past midlife and is in marvelous health, has a lovely family and home, and is independently wealthy. He is the outward epitome of the American success story. And so we ask ourselves: Is his abundance and good reputation in the community a sign of God's blessing? Not to those who know him best!

While the pattern of blessings and curses for the people of Israel as spelled out in our Scripture lesson seems particularly clear, we dare not generalize from it. Scripture offers a great deal of evidence that not all suffering can be considered punishment for sin. The Book of Job is a classic reminder of this truth. In spite of his suffering, Job was confident of his innocence of any wrongdoing and committed himself to wholehearted trust in God. The prophets Jeremiah and Isaiah viewed suffering not as punishment, but as God's training through which the sufferer would be led into a deeper experience of God's love and goodness.

If material blessings are the result of obedience to God, then Jesus—not Aristotle Onassis or J. Paul Getty—should have ended up being the wealthiest man of all time. But Jesus accepted suffering as a way of being faithful to His calling. His suffering was a part of God's plan of redeeming us. And the followers of Jesus are called on to accept suffering as a part of Christian discipleship.

While the Book of Deuteronomy makes a direct connection between sin and suffering, other parts of Scripture make it clear that the issue is much more complex. To be sure, many persons and nations do suffer as a result of their sinfulness, and much suffering is caused by sin. But many good and wonderful people experience deep and painful suffering for which reasonable explanations cannot be found. At the same time, scoundrels among people and nations give every indication of prospering. Perhaps, with Job, we can learn to trust God, no matter what!

A Time for Renewal
(Chapters 29 and 30)

Almost forty years had passed since the Covenant had been given to Moses and the people of Israel by God at Mount Sinai (Horeb). To the Hebrews, forty years also meant an entire generation, and, as far as we can tell, none of the people who had been present at Sinai, except Joshua and Caleb, were allowed to enter the Promised Land. This made the renewal of that Covenant important to the people camped on the plains of Moab. In these two chapters, we have the third major address of Moses to the people of Israel, leading to what appears to be a Covenant oath in 30:11–20.

Not long ago, I was guest speaker at a conference being held at one of the many camp and conference facilities in the mountains of Southern California. This particular place has special meaning for me, for it was there, in 1947, that I made a decision and a public commitment to leave my job in engineering and begin preparing to be an ordained minister.

Now, forty years later, in the stillness of a quiet evening, alone with God, I stood on the very spot where I had witnessed to that covenant. With tears of joy and gratitude, I renewed my covenant with God, grateful for His faithfulness that has always exceeded mine.

The Importance of Remembering

As you read and reflect upon these two chapters, try to recall some significant moment of decision and commitment in your life that might be strengthened by a covenant renewal. Renewal always begins with remembrance. Renewal does not mean a new covenant, but a continuation of the covenant in a new place and time. Remembering God's faithfulness in the past is the basis for renewed commitment and hope for the future.

In spite of their hardness of heart and perpetual lack of vision, God had led the Hebrews out of Egypt and through the wilderness. They had experienced "signs, and . . . great miracles" (29:3) in their liberation. For forty years, God had preserved them under adverse circumstances in the desert, keeping their clothing and even their sandals from wearing out (29:5). As they entered the Transjordan area, God went before them, defeating Sihon and Og, the kings of Heshbon and Bashan (29:7). In remembering God's faithful love and care, they would find the basis of renewal.

In a time when we feel so strongly the need for renewal in our churches, we will benefit by first remembering the faithfulness of God in our own personal histories. Unfortunately, we tend to remember our difficult times so clearly at the expense of recalling the blessings.

A United People

Let your imagination enable you to join the celebrative gathering described in 29:10–15. What a thrill it must have been to stand there with the leaders and members of all the tribes—elders, officers, men, women, children, servants. After forty years of waiting and anticipation, the Promised Land was in sight. Excitement had to be at a fever pitch as they remembered the signs and miracles and looked ahead with expectancy. What a time for renewal!

But the renewing of the covenant with God also included those who were not standing there. The Hebrews and other ancient peoples considered tribal solidarity to be most important. They were united as one with their ancestors and their descendants. So they accepted responsibility for what their forebears had done. And they would be making the renewal for their descendants. They were aware that the actions of every individual had consequences that affected them all, and perhaps most significantly, the future generations.

A Contemporary Conflict

Here is a concept sadly lacking in our Western twentieth-century culture. Our extreme emphasis on individualism and pluralism is virtually the opposite of the Hebrew model. Individualism insists that the highest value is self-fulfillment. Pluralism insists that we allow others to express themselves however they wish, as long as they don't harm anyone else. But our strategies for self-fulfillment and free expression are backfiring. Perceptive observers of contemporary culture, such as Daniel Yankelovich and Robert Bellah, have sounded the alarm on the destructive effects of individualism on our social well-being.

The conflict between individualistic pluralism and social well-being is painfully apparent in the tensions we are experiencing in dealing with the AIDS epidemic. On the one extreme are those who insist on individual rights to the exclusion of social responsibility. Any efforts to restrain the sexual behavior of AIDS carriers is opposed in the name of personal freedom. On the other extreme are those who would sacrifice the rights of individuals to dignity and respect by isolating AIDS carriers from virtually all normal activities and relationships.

Here we must exercise great caution in applying the Bible to a present crisis. There is little question in my mind that the Hebrews would have treated contemporary AIDS carriers the same way they treated lepers or adulterers—by isolative destruction or outright death. Their strong sense of tribal solidarity simply required the removal of all sources of contamination and sin. For them, individual rights were not a consideration in matters of social well-being.

A New Dimension

It was Jesus who brought the new dimension of personal care into the faith of the people of the Bible. Far from diminishing the full meaning of the Law, Jesus heightened it by His insistence on the value of every individual. A new sense of God's love as compassion for every person struck fire in the hearts of those who came to know and follow Jesus. And yet, He never relaxed their sense of solidarity with the whole human race.

While we in the Western world have used Jesus as the champion of individualism and even pluralism, we have neglected His emphasis on our responsibility for one another, and indeed for all of creation.

The Future Challenge

It is the judgment of many people that Western civilization faces a challenge to its very existence. Our future depends on our ability to maintain a healthy respect for the value and the rights of every individual, while at the same time recovering a sense of social responsibility. We need a keen sense of awareness that our actions and behaviors here and now have great consequences for future generations.

A Repetition of the Curse and Blessing Pattern

The pattern of curse and blessing is repeated in the last part of Chapter 29 and the first part of Chapter 30 (29:16–30:10). Here the responsibility of the individual is stressed, with the insistence that the entire nation will suffer the consequences of the sins of individuals. It is all too true that the innocent suffer with the guilty.

But blessing is always promised to those who return to God. Even if they are to be driven out into "captivity" (30:3), which indeed they were, God will bring them back, if only they are willing to return (30:8). The Hebrew word for the act of repenting is best translated "to turn." God is always seen as "the waiting Father," so powerfully portrayed in the parable of the Prodigal Son (Luke 15), longing for His son to return. The good news is eternal: God is always eager to welcome those who return to Him.

The Promise of God's Presence

Moses now comes to the driving conclusion of his third and final address in Deuteronomy (30:11–20). Perhaps at this point the people of Israel were somewhat discouraged, feeling that even turning back to God in a total renewal of the Covenant was much too demanding and difficult. But with pastoral sensitivity, Moses now delivered one of the most beautiful messages in all of biblical literature.

To renew one's relationship with God is "not hidden from thee [too difficult or too mysterious], neither is it far off" (30:11). Moses assures his listeners that God's Word is not elusive or in some far off place (30:12–13). Then comes his ringing assurance, "But the word is very nigh unto thee [near you], in thy mouth, and in thy heart, that thou mayest do it" (30:14).

Here is the great promise for all time—spirituality is not some unreachable goal reserved only for the spiritual elite. To be spiritual does not require gurus or saints to show us the way. Instead, God is near and available to all who are willing to turn to Him.

In one of his greatest statements (Rom. 10:6–13), Paul quoted these verses from Deuteronomy, concluding "that if thou shalt confess with thy mouth the Lord Jesus, and shalt believe in thine heart that God hath raised him from the dead, thou shalt be saved. For with the heart man believeth unto righteousness; and with the mouth confession is made unto salvation" (Rom. 10:9–10). The Word of God is always very near, waiting to be confessed, waiting to be obeyed, waiting to be lived.

The Choice

In the presence of the Word of God, the choice is always between "life and good, and death and evil" (30:15). To choose God is to live. To reject Him is to die. This is much more than a localized message to some folks camped in Moab over three thousand years ago. It is a message with timely implications for us all. Yet it is difficult for us to keep this choice in focus. With so many appeals offering us the good life, we need to discipline ourselves to remember that to live means loving God, obeying Him, and holding steadily to Him (30:20).

The Change in Leadership (Chapters 31–34)

With the end of Chapter 30 the three great messages of Moses are history. The final four chapters of the Book of Deuteronomy move us rapidly toward the future. First, though, Moses has a special message for his people.

Moses Prepares the People for His Death

Moses now shares with the people he has led faithfully for more than forty years his realization that death is near (31:1–6). The old vigor is not there any more. And he reminds his listeners of the Lord's earlier word, "Thou shalt not go over this Jordan" (31:1).

But Moses' attitude is upbeat. There's no doom and gloom in his words as he assures his people that God will go with them into Canaan. God will give them victory. Then he closes his special message to them with a challenge and a promise that have continued to ring across the centuries, "Be strong and of a good courage, fear not, nor be afraid of them [the

Canaanites]: for the Lord thy God, he it is that doth go with thee; he will not fail thee, nor forsake thee" (31:6). There is a solid ring of victory even in the awareness of his approaching death. Moses has accepted the reality of what is about to happen.

Accepting death is something we find difficult to do. Instead, our culture seems to want to deny death. As a clergyman I'm frequently called on to visit with dying people. I'm naturally expected to bring words of faith and comfort, both to the dying person and to the family. But my task is often complicated by the unwillingness of either the patient or the family to face the realities of death. Many times I've been intercepted before entering the patient's room with a comment like this one, "Mary doesn't know she's dying, and we don't want to frighten or discourage her"—meaning, "Don't you dare bring up the subject of death."

Or sometimes when I'm alone with the patient I'm told, "Pastor, I don't think I'm going to make it, but I don't want to talk about this with my wife. It's just too much for her to handle right now."

Then, there's a third scenario in which everyone, including the patient, knows very well that death is close. At the same time, though, everybody seems committed to be cheerful, positive, and upbeat. It's almost as if they believe that by saying all the right things, healing and recovery will come. But this is still a tragic denial of death which robs it of meaning and dignity. How much better to confront death with the acceptance of its reality and the hope of our life with God.

I remember so well the last time I saw my father. He was dying of cancer, and my mother told me by telephone that the time was short. I asked her then if she and my father had talked about his approaching death. She said they hadn't. In fact, she expressed doubt that he was aware of the seriousness of his illness.

All during my airline flight to Florida I debated about whether or not I should initiate the conversation with Dad about the seriousness of his condition. The more I thought about it, the more torn up I was.

When I arrived at the hospital a nurse told me that my father had refused medication that morning because he wanted "to be able to talk clearly" with his son. When I entered his room, he greeted me with these words, "Gary, I know I'm dying, and you know I'm dying—let's talk."

We did! Like we never had before. We spoke openly of our love and respect for each other. We shared our faith in Christ and our belief in eternal life. And we prayed together. These were things we hadn't done quite that way before.

I'll treasure to my dying day the memory of hugging him as we said goodbye, and I'll never forget his words that followed me into the corridor, "If I don't see you again, I'll see you there!"

Dad drifted peacefully into a coma that very night and died a few days later. Over the years Dad had given me many wonderful gifts, including life itself. But the greatest gift he ever gave me was in the hospital room—the gift of affirming life in the process of dying. "Thanks, Dad, I'll see you there!"

This was the legacy Moses now gave the people of Israel on this occasion. Yes, earlier on Mount Pisgah he had argued and pleaded with God to be allowed to march into Canaan with his people (3:23–29)—all to no avail. Now we see him calmly preparing everyone for his death and for the next chapter in their lives.

Moses Prepares Joshua for His Future

Next, Moses directs his remarks to Joshua, his heir apparent (31:7–8). Again, the promise is certain—be strong and courageous for the Lord will be with you. Moses assures Joshua out of long experience that God will never fail him. Here we see Moses at his noblest as he prepares Joshua to be his successor.

Instructions for the Priests

Moses then gave a special set of instructions to the priests (31:9–13). Their responsibility was to see to it the people knew the Law. And every seven years was to be a time of renewal—a time of rehearing the provisions of the Covenant. But it was more than just a time of "hearing"; it was a time of learning, of recommitment, of renewal.

192

There is a very pertinent application for us here, I believe. For example, I know of two churches in Southern California that have held formal services in which everybody present renewed their membership vows. I think this is a healthy exercise. Our church membership vows are sacred before the Lord, and are worthy of renewal.

Joshua Is Commissioned and the People Are Warned

Moses once again hears from the Lord—this time for Moses and Joshua to meet Him at the Tabernacle (31:14–15). The Deuteronomy writer only tells us that the Lord appeared "in the pillar of cloud," but it was in this dramatic meeting that Joshua's future was confirmed.

Then, we're told, the Lord spoke to Moses again. This time the warning was given of Israel's future rebellion (31:16–29). In anticipation of that time the Deuteronomy writer tells us that God instructed Moses to "write this song"—this rule for living—so it could be referred to in the days to come. Moses obeyed these instructions, gave Joshua his final commission, and then handed what he had written to the Levites for preservation.

The Song of Moses

In the last verse of Chapter 31, the writer prepares us for what is commonly referred to as "The Song of Moses" (32:1–43). This type of song was quite common among the people of the ancient world. It is actually more like a court case or lawsuit than a musical number. In this action, the sovereign power— God—is confronting an errant vassal for breaking a treaty.

The Song opens with a declaration of the majesty and character of God (32:1–4), much as a court case would open with a declaration of authority. Then in verse 5 we have this initial statement of the case: "They have corrupted themselves . . . they are a perverse and crooked generation." And in verse 6 we have the preliminary interrogation—three questions stated in rapid sequence—(1) Is this the way you repay the Lord? (2) Isn't He your father? (3) Didn't He make you a nation?

The third movement of the Song (32:7–14) is a

rehearsal of the past acts of God in Israel's behalf—His selection of Israel as His special people (32:8–9), the miraculous deliverance of Israel from Egyptian bondage (32:10–12); and God's gracious gift to them of the Land of Promise—Canaan (32:13–14).

Next comes the specific indictment of the people of Israel (32:15–18). Despite the overwhelming goodness of God, *Jeshurun*—a title for Israel—has become fat and overfed and has gone after strange gods. On the surface the meaning here may seem a bit obscure. However, what we have is a picture, all too common even today, of people who become comfortable and "fat" with material abundance and then turn to their own particular brand of false gods.

Continuing the analogy of a court case, after the indictment has been given, the sentence is passed (32:19–25). God is pictured as hiding His face from them, withholding His favor from them. The judgments of hunger, pestilence, destruction, beasts, serpents, the sword, and sheer terror remind us of the curses listed in Chapter 28.

In verses 26 through 35 we have a word picture of God deliberating with Himself, reconsidering His judgment because of how it would be interpreted by Israel's enemies. This opens the door to hope, and Israel's ultimate deliverance is promised. A final promise of deliverance is reiterated in verses 36–42, and Israel is called upon once again to worship God (32:43).

Moses, with Joshua by his side, then urges the people of Israel to be attentive to the words of the Lord and to obey all the words of the Law (32:44–47). Obedience is serious business, because it means life (verse 47).

The Lord Speaks to Moses Again about His Death

Once again, the Lord warns Moses that the time of his death is near (32:48–52). Mount Nebo, also referred to as Pisgah, has been identified as a peak in the Abarim or Moab range. Located about nine miles northeast of the Dead Sea, Mount Nebo affords a commanding view of the entire Jordan valley. It was from Nebo's peak that Moses got his first glimpse of the Promised Land.

A view of Mount Nebo near the peak.

In Chapter 33 we have the poetic blessing of Moses given to the tribes of Israel. The parting words and blessings of family heads and tribal leaders were regarded with reverence in ancient times. Such blessings were considered to be irrevocable, as with a modern will, and were thought to be a determining factor in future events.

The blessing begins with a brief introduction which highlights God's revealing of Himself to the people of Israel in the wilderness. His love for the people is celebrated and affirmed (33:2–5).

The body of the blessing (verses 6–25) speaks to each tribe in turn, beginning with Reuben. Reuben's blessing refers to this tribe's obscurity in the future. The blessing for the tribe of Judah in verse 7 relates

Moses Blesses the Israelites

to military success. As the lead tribe in any march, Judah would be the first in battle.

The blessing for the Levites refers to the Urim and Thummim, a term we met in our earlier studies in the Book of Leviticus. Most students of the Bible believe these to have been two flat rocks with Urim inscribed on one side and Thummim on the other. In seeking guidance, these would have been thrown like dice. For instance, if both sides came up Urim, the answer might have been no; if both sides came up Thummim, the answer might have been yes. This, of course, is only conjecture, except we do know that these were a means of obtaining guidance. The tribe of Levi is commended for having been faithful at Massah and Meribah (Exod. 17:1–7; Num. 20:2–13), and is called to be teachers of the Law to all of Israel.

Benjamin is blessed in verse 12 as being "beloved of the Lord." Joseph (the combined tribes of Ephraim and Manasseh) receives the longest and most lavish blessing (33:13–17). It is obvious that Joseph was regarded as the strongest and most exceptional of all the tribes. The remaining tribes receive their particular blessing in verses 18 through 25.

Moses' grand hymn of blessing concludes with a powerful affirmation of God's love and care for His people—the children of Israel. Most certainly, the people of God in every century since these words were spoken have found strength and courage in these marvelous words that were almost the last Moses is recorded as having spoken, "The eternal God is thy refuge, and underneath are the everlasting arms" (33:27).

The Death of Moses

The story of Moses' death (Chapter 34) is told simply and without fanfare. This is the third reference in Deuteronomy to Pisgah peak as the place of Moses' death (cf. 3:23–29; 32:48–52). It's a touching scene when we read between the lines. Moses makes his way to the peak of Nebo, some 2700 feet high. There we read, "The Lord shewed him all the land," from the Negev in the south to Dan in the north, from the palm trees of Jericho across the Jordan to the Great Sea in the west (the Mediterranean).

Then we read that "Moses *the servant of the Lord* died there in the land of Moab, according to the word of the Lord" (34:5, italics mine). The people of Israel mourned for thirty days, and command was shifted to Joshua.

Moses, the great liberator, the servant of the Lord is now labeled a prophet by the Deuteronomy writer, "And there arose not a prophet since in Israel like unto Moses, whom the Lord knew face to face" (34:10). But he was more than a prophet; he was God's spokesman at the birth of a nation.

The chief human character throughout all of our studies—God's spokesman at a critical period in biblical history—was this man Moses. It was his faith that held the people of Israel steady through the Exodus from Egypt to the plains of Moab east of the Jordan River. And it is his faith that stands as a prime example for us in these closing years of the twentieth century. What he believed was important then—and now.

A Brief Summary of Moses' Faith

1. *Moses believed that Israel's God, Yahweh, was a God of history.*
   In contrast to the capricious pagan gods of all time, Israel's God was and is intimately involved in human affairs. He is a God of purpose.
2. *Moses believed that God took the initiative in the events of the Exodus and in all of Israel's life.*
   From his dramatic meeting with God at the burning bush in the desert, Moses saw Him act through the confrontation with Pharaoh in Egypt, the Exodus, and the separation of the waters at the sea. And Moses knew that it was through God's initiative that the Sinai Covenant was given, and the people of Israel were prepared and positioned for their occupation of the Land of Promise.
3. *Moses believed that only the God of Israel was to be worshiped.*
   In contrast to the polytheism practiced in Egypt and the ancient Near East only Israel's God was

completely trustworthy and to be worshiped.
"Thou shalt have no other gods before me."

4. *Moses believed that the "children of Israel" were chosen by God to live directly under His guidance and in obedience to His will.*

It was through the Sinai Covenant they saw themselves as a chosen people, called to be priests who would be guided by God to represent Him and a new way of life in Canaan. It is through Christ that we as Christians are a chosen people and a royal priesthood.

5. *Moses believed that God lived in the midst of His people and acted in both judgment and mercy.*

In contrast to the far off and indifferent pagan gods, Moses' God stayed close to His people. In response to their lapses into the evils of disobedience and polytheism, the Exodus people were forbidden entrance into Canaan and died in the wilderness. But in mercy God graciously gave them the commandments and the Law and led the new generation into their Land of Promise.

6. *Moses believed that God intended for the people of Israel to influence and lead all people and nations to obedience and loyalty to the one true God.*

They were to be the fulfillment of God's original covenant with Abraham (Gen. 12:1–2)— "Through you all of the people of the earth shall be blessed." They were to settle in Canaan and become a missionary people who modeled obedience and worship before their neighbors and lead them to a relationship with God. To believers of all time Jesus said, "But ye shall receive power, after that the Holy Ghost is come upon you: and ye shall be witnesses unto

(TOP) A view from the top of Mount Nebo toward the north end of the Dead Sea and the south end of the Jordan valley.
(BOTTOM) As Moses looked a little further north from the peak of Nebo, he would have picked up this view of the rich Jordan valley in the Land of Promise.

me both in Jerusalem, and in all Judaea, and in Samaria, and unto the uttermost part of the earth."

Almighty God, Thank You for being my refuge, for upholding me with Your everlasting arms. AMEN.

WHAT THIS SCRIPTURE MEANS TO ME
Deuteronomy 29—34

Blaise Pascal, a famous French scientist who lived in the seventeenth century, determined to write a book someday. He envisioned writing a great theological work, and so he collected his thoughts and ideas, jotting them down as they came to him.

He planned to organize these notes, to weave them together into a work of enormous importance and impact. But before he could start his project, he died.

After his death, as people were going through his letters and his work, they recognized the value of his notes. They published these ideas just as they were—bits and pieces of wisdom.

Even though it was never "finished," Pascal's *Pensées* (French for "thoughts") has become a classic, read by millions of people over the centuries.

In our lesson, Moses has reached the end of his life. God leads him up to the top of Mount Pisgah where he sees the Promised Land spread out beneath him. Like Pascal, Moses sees the vision of the completion of his life's work just out of his reach. He knows he is about to die.

This lesson spoke to me in several powerful ways. One of my first impulses was to think, "How sad that Moses wasn't able to go into the Promised Land, especially after everything he did for the people and for God."

Then several other things occurred to me. First of all, the vision of the Promised Land itself was a gift from God. The rest of the original group from Egypt had died because of disobedience, but Moses was allowed to stand at the threshold and look out over the land his people would finally claim. Though he didn't get to go personally, he did get to see it.

Also, I realized that if we truly give our lives to God, we become His instruments, no matter what the outcome. God used Moses for His purposes for many years. It was the daily, hourly relationship Moses had with God that mattered, rather than whether or not Moses participated in the ultimate goal.

Sometimes, like Pascal, we set our sights on accomplishing some very worthwhile task. But then, if things don't work out the way we think they should, we feel we have failed. Yet God may have something different in mind. We can't measure our success as Christians by any worldly standard.

I have seen this happen in my own life. One year, I taught English to young foreign students in a poverty-stricken school. I started out with the idealistic goal that all the students would be fluent in English by the end of the year.

However, I didn't count on the students' resistance to being in America. I didn't count on families who encouraged them to speak their native language. I didn't count on their truancy, or their use of drugs. Every day was a struggle.

By the time I left the job, I felt I had failed miserably. Only a handful of students had made progress. The rest were not much more literate in English than they were on the first day of school.

Yet at the end, I received lots and lots of letters and gifts from the students—more than I have ever received since as a teacher. As I look back on the experience, perhaps God placed me there with a different goal in mind. I loved my students, and I think they knew they were loved. Perhaps that was more important than their learning English.

The message in this lesson, for me, is that when we give our lives to God, we become His instruments. We have to give up our own goals and visions to let Him use us for His purposes. Like Moses, we must walk day by day with God, leaving the final results of our lives up to Him.